Foreword

Mary W. Davis

EXECUTIVE DIRECTOR
AMERICAN CENTER FOR DESIGN

WITH THIS, the American Center for Design's Seventeenth 100 Show, I've now had the experience of seeing the competition through from start to finish. We began by inviting just the right chair, Rick Poynor, who in turn invited just the right jury: Stephen Doyle, Laurie Haycock Makela, and Rudy VanderLans. We sent out Rudy's wonderfully American poster calling for entries, watched the UPS delivery persons stagger into our office with heaped hand trucks and armloads of entries, saw all 1,700 submissions laid out for inspection, witnessed the first round of cuts, the second round of cuts, over which our earnest jury truly agonized, then listened as they explained the reasoning behind each one of their choices.

In the following essays and notes, the fact that in this competition our jurors are asked to make their own individual decisions, working as design curators rather than through attempting consensus, is discussed by each juror. Curating is, of course, common enough in other milieus; curators in the art world wield considerable influence in shaping individual careers and furthering critical concepts through choices and juxtapositions of artists' work. A fundamental difference, however, is that art curators have all the world to choose from; any artist, any work by that artist, and in some cases work created specifically for an individual show.

Our curator/jurors have only the pieces that, for whatever reason, a designer has chosen to enter in this competition. Granted, when looking at what seem to be hundreds of tables covered with literally thousands of entries, one doesn't really sense that lack of material will be a problem. My point, though, is that we receive so many entries that are at such a consistently high level of proficiency and creativity that our jurors really do have the opportunity to make their own critical and conceptual points. For that we thank the thousands of entrants to this competition.

The 100 Show competition, exhibition, and this publication represent this organization's primary avenue of investigation into the interest area that we refer to as "Next?". One of the few specific instructions that the jurors are given is to watch the horizon, to focus as far away as possible in order to spot the next design wave. It's somewhat ironic, then, to realize that the actual process involved in doing this competition is reassuringly, perhaps somewhat old-fashionedly, physical. The jurors communicate by talking together in the same room, not by teleconference, not by e-mail. They make their choices by looking at and holding the real things in their hands, not videos, facsimiles, or CD-ROMs.

Laurie refers in her notes to the general paucity of work in emerging media submitted to this year's competition. We can be certain, however, that increasingly these new media will become the proving ground for designers. Who knows? The physical realities of this year's 100 Show may be part of a way of doing things that we will look back on longingly and nostalgically when, ten years from now, we conduct our competition and lives in an increasingly virtual fashion.

In the meantime though, the whole process — competition, chair, jury, entries, exhibition and this publication — remains delightfully physical. Chair and jurors have the chance to get to know each other in person, and jurors make their decisions using their hands and eyes, as well as their brains. As you will see in the documentation that follows, their choices are informed and thoughtful.

It all comes around again with our next competition, not long from now. Stay tuned.

The 100^{+2} show

The seventeenth annual
OF THE AMERICAN CENTER FOR DESIGN

Design Year in Review

ACD Board

© 1995 American Center for Design

Published by AMERICAN CENTER FOR DESIGN, 233 East Ontario Street, Chicago, Illinois 60611, USA

Distributed to the trade by WATSON-GUPTILL PUBLICATIONS, 1515 Broadway,
New York, New York 10036, USA

Distributed outside the U.S. and Canada by RotoVision SA, 9, route Suisse,
CH-1295 Mies, Switzerland

Available through mail order from EMIGRE, 4475 D Street, Sacramento, California 95819, USA, and from
AMERICAN CENTER FOR DESIGN, 233 East Ontario Street, Chicago, Illinois 60611, USA.

ISBN 0-8230-6450-6

Printed in the U.S.A.

Editor: *Rob Dewey*. Book Design and Photography: *Emigre*.

For information about membership in American Center for Design,
call us toll free at 1-800-257-8657.

The American Center for Design is a member-based organization of design professionals, educators and
students. In addition to promoting excellence in design education and practice, it serves as a national
center for the accumulation and dissemination of information regarding design and its role in our culture
and economy.

The Dice are **Rolling**

Rick Poynor

CHAIR
SEVENTEENTH ANNUAL 100 SHOW

THE 100 SHOW has emerged in the last few years as one of the most insightful and stimulating of design competitions. While the traditional com-
petition-as-beauty-pageant assumes jurors will be sufficiently similar in
their judgments to arrive at a natural consensus, the 100 Show encourages jurors to find their own path through the submitted entries, to form
personal conclusions, and in effect "curate" their selections. Jurors are
given the opportunity to write about the work, while the chair and other
essayists explore themes arising from the show. The book's yearly changes in design and format reflect the shifting perspectives of the people
who put it together. All of this makes the 100 Show unusually valuable
as a report on new developments in American design, and it is a book I
look out for in the London book shops.

 So I was delighted to be asked by Katherine McCoy to chair the
1994 show, but also a little surprised. I welcomed the opportunity of collaborating with designers whose work I admire and the chance to see
so many examples of American graphic design in the original. (Whatever
else you might say about design competitions this is the single most compelling reason for attending them.) On the other hand, there are still
sufficiently few non-designers such as myself taking a close interest in
graphic design for me to feel like an interloper on occasions when I have
been involved — as a juror — in competitions in which the brightest and
best join ranks to judge their fellow professionals. Twice an interloper
in the case of the 100 Show, since my view of American graphic design,
much as it interests me, is that of an outsider looking in.

 One thing you quickly realize when chairing this show is that the
dice were loaded from the moment they were thrown. The selection of
the dice — that is the selection of *you*, the chair — presupposes a certain
frame of reference and thus a certain kind of jury. The chair has no vote,

but the power to select the jury, your first responsibility, encourages
a form of voting by proxy, which potentially works to the advantage of
both chair and show. The chair can further load the dice to reflect
the range of his or her own concerns and interests, while the show gains
a diversity of viewpoints that the traditional competition's demand for
consensus will inevitably stifle.

This, at least, is the theory. Almost too neatly, the geographical
spread of my chosen jurors corresponded to their relative positions
on the spectrum of design possibilities. New Yorker Stephen Doyle — re-
nowned for urbane, witty, word-conscious solutions — would cover the
intelligent end of the corporate mainstream. Drawing on her wide experience as design director of the Walker Art Center, Minneapolis, Laurie
Haycock Makela would bring a sharp eye and understanding to the
institutional entries. And who better equipped to detect the first quiv-
ering signs of emerging experimentation than Californian mentor of the
typographic avant-garde, Rudy VanderLans?

There is, of course, at least a shred of truth in these simplifica-
tions and some evidence for this can be found in the way people voted.
If Stephen Doyle and Rudy VanderLans would seem on paper to be the
furthest apart in their sympathies, then this receives a small measure of
confirmation in the selections made by two designers, where they have
the fewest overlaps — eight, compared to 16 for Stephen and Laurie, and
11 for Laurie and Rudy. It was Stephen, though, rather than the others,
who selected a David Carson project[1], while Rudy emerged as an admirer   1 / SEE PAGE 81
of professional "hyper-mastery" in sober-sided entries that would make
some of *Emigre*'s wilder collaborators pause in wonder.

Jurors proved wayward in a more fundamental sense. It is striking
given the quantity of designs (some 1,700 pieces), the supposed diversity
of the jurors, and the encouragement to go their own way what a large
measure of agreement remains. "Our biggest concern," wrote Katherine
McCoy, chairing the show in 1991, "was that in spite of their varied backgrounds and biases these three individuals would agree too much and
choose the same pieces." This concern has proved to be well grounded.
Katherine's jury jointly selected only six pieces (12 if you count seven
Beach Culture spreads separately). The following year, with Michael
Bierut as chair, this jumped to 22, with 40 more pieces chosen by two jurors — a category of selection not available to Katherine's jury. "Despite
our differing backgrounds and sensibilities, we seemed to have shared
frame of reference and similar criteria for evaluating the work," noted
Alexander Isley. Last year Ellen Lupton's jury achieved consensus on
18 pieces, with 49 chosen by two designers. This year the figures are
down — 13 by all jurors, 35 by two jurors — but still approximately half
of the total.

At this stage in its evolution the 100 Show seems caught between two styles of competition. This will be more apparent this year from the way the selections are structured than it was in the two previous books, where the selections took the form of undivided alphabetical runs. My principle reason for making this change is to reinstate the still valuable idea of the individually curated show. I hope it will be easier to see the threads that link Laurie's, Stephen's, and Rudy's individual selections and what (if anything) sets them apart from each other.

A large measure of agreement nevertheless persists; so how do we explain it? I believe it is an inevitable consequence of the format and organization of the show (and other shows like it). The ticking clock, enormous pile of designs to be sifted, and their typological variety obliges jurors to respond at the simplest and most accessible level — the formal — and to favor work which departs most obviously from the formal average. It is hardly surprising that professional designers with core values in common (Alexander Isley's "shared frame of reference") will make similar judgments at this level. What the 100 Show needs to implement, if it wants to avoid this, is a mechanism within the competition for probing the deeper levels of a design and allowing more personal criteria to be brought to bear on the entries. In his notes, Rudy VanderLans gives a vivid account, from the point of view of someone acting as a juror for the first time, of the issues he felt could not be assessed in the time available: economical use of resources, effectiveness in problem solving, and social or cultural significance. Laurie Haycock Makela proposes forms of contribution to design practice, such as lectures, teaching and exhibitions, which are no less deserving of acknowledgment and award than formal invention.

The 100 Show is remarkable for the freedom it gives chairs, jurors, and essayists to explore the limitations of the competition format and, ultimately, to question the very basis of its existence. Two years ago, Michael Rock concluded an exhaustive critique with the suggestion that the competition might call for work on specific themes, allowing the jury to make more thorough comparisons and truly curate the show. Even if such a sweeping redefinition of the entry criteria is not possible, jurors could still base their individual selections on more tightly defined genres and themes within the show as a whole — books, magazines, design for cultural institutions or the corporate sector, and so on. It is clear, though, that the show cannot make the same criticisms of itself indefinitely: it must either change in the way that its participants suggest, or accept its own limitations, dig in its heels, and stick to its established strengths.

My approach as chair was in part a reaction to these still unresolved issues. The book's annual changes of format suggest a dialectic and,

9

though I enjoyed the bookishness of last year's volume, it seemed truer
to my own role as a journalist, and appropriate to the way the show
functions as a report, to give it a more magazine-like quality this year. In
a real sense, competitions are like journalism. They offer the excitement
of immediacy: *this is how it was in 1994.* They try to tell the story now,
while it is happening, working as best they can with the materials at
hand, in the certain knowledge that things will be left out and that the
full story may not emerge until long after the event (if anyone is still
interested). Competitions should be conducted as rigorously as possible,
but it is probably hoping for too much to expect a format born out of
professional celebration to bear a critical burden that is better carried
by other forms of writing and commentary — magazines, journals, books,
exhibitions — where the researcher is not bound by who chose (or could
afford) to enter, and by the competition's intrinsic need to slice up the
evidence into annual packages.

Ordinarily, the chair designs the book, the exhibition and periph-
erals and I am indebted to Rudy VanderLans for agreeing to take on these
tasks on my behalf: it has been a chance to carry on the dialogue between our magazines by other means. Previous essayists have addressed
the show's institutional dimension and process, and the language of its
judgments; this year, to make the essay series a triptych, I asked
Véronique Vienne to take a notebook into the jury room, observe the
judging process, and record for posterity what actually went on in there.

The 100 Show's self-elected mission is to spot new trends. But
graphic design, while it has something in common with fashion's wandering hemlines, is not driven quite so strictly, or abruptly, by the seasons.
How much does it matter, in any case, if there was a rush of enthusiasm
this year for rough textures simply printed, or cool spiral bindings? The
pluralism of 100 Show entries is the most striking single feature about
them, as it has been for several years. Some shifts of emphasis were certainly apparent in the jury's selections, but were these to do with the
chemistry of this particular trio, or some wider tendency or mood?

Ray Gun was a unanimous selection last year and the jurors pre-
dicted annual reports this year full of Carson clones. On the evidence
here that has not happened, while David Carson himself was largely
overlooked by this jury. They were equally unengaged by the kind of
layering and complexity — "typo-technics," as Stephen Doyle calls it —
that not so long ago was the last word in modishness. Meanwhile other,
less familiar names kept surfacing: Rebeca Méndez[2] of Art Center College
of Design, Pasadena; ReVerb[3], the five-strong team from Los Angeles;
Portland-based Johnson & Wolverton[4]; J. Abbott Miller[5] of Design Writing
Research in New York. What links these very different designers is their
thoughtful engagement with content and the way they shun the

2 / SEE PAGES 38, 92, 102

3 / SEE PAGES 39, 66, 100, 108

4 / SEE PAGES 42, 55, 99

5 / SEE PAGES 47, 53, 58

crowd-pleasing devices of fashionable style. And yet a similar, emergent seriousness was discerned by 1991's jury. As fast as graphic design seems to move these days, it still takes several years for it to become evident whether or not a fundamental reorientation has occurred.

A visitor sees a different story, anyway. The projects that stood out most for me were often from client areas that receive little design attention in Great Britain and Europe, or attention of a highly predictable kind. It is hard to imagine the London office of Amnesty International accepting anything as edgy or extreme as Johnson & Wolverton's design for American Amnesty's *Say* magazine (shortlisted, but not finally selected). An art catalogue such as Susan Silton of SoS's design for a Kim Abeles exhibition at Santa Monica Museum of Art[6] is simply without precedent in Britain. Even if a designer were confident enough to propose this degree of parodic playfulness, the artist were to approve it, and the sponsoring institution could be persuaded to accept such a break with the conventional catalogue, the budget would not be available to realize it in such exact and loving detail.

6 / SEE PAGE 96

So I am happy to admit it. When Rudy VanderLans advises himself to settle for "sheer wonderment," I know exactly what he means, and so does any designer. No matter how many times you say "showing great work isn't enough (and what *is* great work anyway?)", you come back to the fact that designers are drawn to the profession because great work is what they love to look at and want to make. The responsibility may weigh heavily on a juror struggling to find adequate criteria to meet the task of selection, but most jurors of any competition, if asked, would do it again. Personally, I think this jury was crazy not to have selected anything from the front pages of *Wired*, which has inspired whole magazines in imitation in Europe, but that is entirely their privilege.

In the end, the dice fall where they will. This is their show.

Rituals in a Jury Room

Véronique Vienne

WHERE THE JURORS
— NOT THE ENTRIES —
CAME UNDER SCRUTINY

Day One

THE FIRST THING I did when I saw the rows of tables laden with some of the show's 1,700 entries was wring my hands. Standing next to me, Rudy VanderLans was running nervous fingers through his blond hair. Laurie Haycock Makela took a deep breath and began to fidget with the pleats of her skirt. Stephen Doyle smiled cryptically and tightened his grip on his coffee cup.

Whoever said graphic design was a mental discipline? Faced with a roomful of printed material, our initial reaction was intensely physical. A new palpable awareness made the tip of our fingers tingle. Senses sharpened by the smell of ink and the sight of fibrous paper, we circled the tables like hungry predators. Visual curiosity is fed by a delicious tactile craving.

Outside, through the cafeteria bay windows, the kaleidoscopic Chicago skyline reflected an ever-changing Western sky. Inside, the landscape was just as variegated. Acre upon acre of prime intellectual real estate — brochures, books, catalogs, journals, magazines, newsletters and reports — reflected the multi-faceted concerns of untold numbers of people, institutions and businesses.

The rules of the game are simple, we are told. The three jurors are independent of each other and can proceed as they want. The first day they are only required to select entries they wish to consider. With colored Post-It notes, they save worthy submissions from being unceremoniously dismissed. The second day they will be invited to edit their selection. A civilized process, the system is designed to foster a sense of nonconformity. This is the land of the free — and the brave.

At first, the three jurors hesitate at the edge of this graphic wilderness. They huddle together in the annual reports and corporate brochures area. "Can we peek at the names of the designers?" asks Laurie.

Véronique Vienne

"Can we talk to each other?" asks Stephen. "Is there money under the entries?" inquires Rudy.

Urged to do as they please, they each go their own way. For a while you only hear the dry flutter of pages, the occasional flapping of a soft cover and the furtive pat of a hand across a piece of paper. Expressive textures combined with a deliberate economy of images give this show an irresistible sensuality. The two-dimensional surface is striving to acquire a three-dimensional status. Commercial publications are disguised as thick artist spiral notebooks. Intricate annual reports masquerade as old-fashioned filing systems. Catalogs are designed to look like unedited manuscripts. You don't simply open a brochure anymore — you peel, unfurl, take apart and unwrap. Gaining access to the written material can be quite a project.

"If you can't figure out what it is," asks Rudy, "is it good or bad?" He is holding in his hand a Chicago Volunteer Legal Services[7] piece that looks like a cross between an accounting ledger and a quaint dog-eared file folder. "It's weird — but maybe it has a fantastic content," he adds. Oblivious of the remaining 1,684 entries, he pulls a red plastic chair, sits down comfortably and proceeds to read the brochure cover to cover.

7 / SEE PAGE 31

Good design can be conducive to bad behavior. While Rudy stubbornly deconstructs the Chicago Volunteer Legal Services brochure, Stephen inspects a local eatery's lunch menu. "It's an electronic macramé of typographical errors," he comments. "No production value — but delightfully under-designed. I wonder if I should order the roasted chicken salad sandwich." Laurie decides to forge ahead — and makes a beeline for the literary journals displayed in the next room. "I have a low tolerance for self-promotion pieces," she remarks, bypassing 20 tables jam-packed with Christmas cards and invitations mixed together with corporate identity program entries. "I'll look at that area after lunch."

Progress is slow — as soon as a table is "judged," it is cleared and fresh new entries are immediately laid out. A Sisyphean labor it is. But the serenity of the support staff is unfaltering. Rick Poynor, who chairs the show, takes unhurried notes. Rob Dewey, ACD's director of communications, operates ominously from backstage. Executive Director Mary Davis hovers like a benevolent figure. The official fly on the wall, I apologize each time I bump into someone. Because of the enormity of the task, everyone acts very cool.

Yet something is definitely amiss. The work submitted cannot be judged at leisure in these conditions. It would take months for a team of experts to give each entry the kind of attention it richly deserves. I check on Rudy, who seems to have given up on the Chicago Volunteer Legal Services brochure and is now engrossed in a portfolio, a sedate catalog of Italian watercolors for the Krannert Art Museum[8]. "Who is this artist Al Held?" he asks me. "Is he important? I like the design of the

8 / SEE PAGE 117

brochure but I don't like his work very much. Does it matter? What's relevant here?" Stephen, over-hearing our conversation, answers without missing a beat: "The only relevant question to ask ourselves is do we want next year's annual reports to look like this?"

Suddenly it occurs to me that the outcome of the weekend will not be the objective selection of the 100 best entries — scrap that idea — but the collective reaffirmation of our commitment to design as a noble and worthy discipline. The judging process is a ritualistic event during which the jurors — not the entries — are coming under scrutiny. The mandate of Rudy, Laurie and Stephen is to define who we are by reaching for universal predicaments concealed under narrative pieces. In order to do the job, the judges must put their idiosyncracies aside, personify their point of view and accept being reduced to stereotypes. The transformation takes place in less than two hours. By 11:00am, Stephen is assuming the role of the corporate type; Rudy impersonates the artiste; Laurie has embraced the part of the new woman.

Dapper Stephen — in Lee jeans, J. Crew polo shirt worn over a white cotton tee, half-deckers and croco belt — is the one who always gets it first. While you are still trying to figure out how to open the brochure, he already has a handle on what it all means. "I wonder how their business is doing," he remarks dryly in front of an over-produced corporate brochure. A slick paper promotion has him wondering if we invent simple-minded problems in order to come up with astute design solutions. He has the gift of the gab. "Scribbles, circumcised typography..." he mutters when inspecting a self-indulgent digitalized graphic exercise. His choices tend to be bookish, handsome and culturally meaningful. He is the Charlie Rose of our profession.

Rudy, who wears his Levi's Euro-style with an olive green twill shirt untucked, white socks and black shoes, makes a point of never taking anything for granted. "I don't know what this is," he says repeatedly. "Are we judging a beauty pageant?" he asks later in all earnest. And then, faced with yet another example of how not to use Template Gothic, one of the popular typefaces he distributes, he quips: "It's funny, I should be happy to see how many people use my products, but all I can think is did they pay for it?" A champion of the playful and the unformatted, he is endlessly fascinated by under-produced, monochromatic conceptual pieces.

Laurie, who stashes her Post-It notes in her bra to keep her hands free, wears a short pleated skirt, a Jeff Koons t-shirt tucked-in, black hose and no shoes. Caring and curious, she wants to know how all these posters, catalogs, reports, t-shirts and invitations have performed for the people they were destined to. "How did it affect the collective energy?" she wonders aloud. "It's too decorative — but maybe that's part of the reason it works," she says of a museum calendar. She is the one who notices that most female names on entry slips identify the "entrant" — the person who mailed the competition — not the "designer" — who will get credit for it. A discussion ensues. Who is Sarah Haun, Pentagram's "entrant"? Jenna Maliza, with Frankfurt Balkind? Sally Howe, who filled so many slips for Jager Di Paola Kemp? Anne Dolan, employed by Duffy Design? For Laurie, no matter what people do, if they are involved, they become an integral part of the process. "These entries reflect a collective mind," she says, "not the intention of a few individuals."

By mid-afternoon, the jurors, now working in synch, have weeded through more than a thousand projects. Stephen's blue stickers are few and far apart. Laurie's green ones earmark community and institutional projects. Rudy's pink slips are everywhere — the editor-in-chief of *Emigre* has adopted a liberal, non-restrictive policy.

In spite of the apparent randomness of the process, new trends are emerging. Tribalism, recognizable by its wild electronic typography and full-bodied color palette, is on the rise — but David Carson has peaked. The snow-boarding industry is still on the leading edge of graphic innovation. Waste management companies make the best clients. Handwriting is still in favor. Honesty and self-parody are critical design ingredients. Education has replaced information — a "show, don't tell" approach is making a big comeback.

Fleeting cultural perceptions, influenced by the electronic media, now affect the way we look at staid printed matter. The first day ends on a sobering note: to monitor the trends and keep up with the shifting taste of clients and audiences, one show a year isn't enough anymore. The way things are going, the American Center for Design should organize seasonal graphic design shows.

Day Two

This morning Rudy wears a white tee; Stephen sports a yellow striped shirt; Laurie dons a Walker Art Center t-shirt with tightly rolled short sleeves. Apostles of the new design testament, they are ready for their ultimate test — the editing down of yesterday's free-wheeling selection. Each juror is allowed about 35 submissions. For Stephen and Laurie, this means refining their philosophy. For Rudy it's a daunting task. He looks pale and confides that he didn't sleep last night. "I don't know that I can do the job," he says.

First comes the exegesis — the exposition — an attempt from our three jurors to create a critical context from which to proceed. Stephen sits down on the edge of a chair, Laurie leans back on a table and Rudy hunkers down, one knee on the floor. The discussion centers around the relevance of the judging process, a phase Rob Dewey views from a distance with a touch of apprehension. All juries, he knows from experience, must sooner or later pass through this painful stage in order to come to terms with their final selection.

Watching them debate the issues of text versus context and individual mandate versus social responsibility is the closest thing to watching three beautiful fish caught in a treacherous nylon net. Rick Poynor looks away. Volunteering students, who have gathered around the group to listen, stare at their shoes. Curiosity incites me to join in the debate — and I soon regret it. No one can alleviate the discomfort that precedes a moment of truth.

The pressure to do the right thing is such that soon the judging process resumes and moves swiftly toward its preordained conclusion. This is a design competition — good taste must prevail in the end.

Nonetheless, the Seventeenth Annual 100 Show is prone to quirkiness. Laurie, Stephen and Rudy are now engaged in tough ethical negotiations intended to protect individual voices, promote relevance and define quality. Collaborative efforts between writers and designers are rewarded; non-elitist projects are favored; weird, homespun and obsessive pieces benefit from a little extra consideration. Chuck Anderson's work is viewed as eccentric. A politically incorrect Mohawk Paper project is severely reprimanded. Visual statements using every trick in the book make no good impression.

After Rudy peels off 36 pink Post-It notes from his original pile of selected entries, the Chicago Volunteer Legal Services brochure is still in the running. A student project, Margo Johnson's *Hybrid Digital Typefaces* book[9], wins everybody's vote. Coca-Cola's generation X OK[10] can, a marketing gimmick, gets the stamp of approval. But the surprise of the show is how good the jurors feel about the most unlikely project, one that does not fit in any category: a handrail for the blind, with directions in Braille tucked out of sight under a slim oak banister[11].

It's the final revenge: the most clearly defined entry features design you can't see but can only touch. An entire weekend spent groping in the dark for valid design standards is redeemed by a single invisible tactile stroke. It makes perfect sense. Like the blind, designers need guidelines in order to find their way around. Each selected piece in the 100 Show is but a raised dot on the seamless surface of our professional practice. Decipher this Braille message, and you'll know where to find the exit door. Competitions are meant to help you look ahead, not over your shoulder.

Before leaving, the jurors shake hands. That contact neutralizes the spell. Rudy wanders out; Laurie rushes to the phone to find out how her child is doing; Stephen gets to make one last comment. "We always want to push design forward," he says, "but we never ask where." We laugh and then are on our way home — back to New York, Minneapolis, San Francisco and London.

9 / SEE PAGE 36

10 / SEE PAGE 128

11 / SEE PAGE 41

Do We Have **Faith?**

Stephen Doyle

Siege

THE CITY OF CHICAGO is under siege. Out on Lake Michigan, a uniformed militia assaults the beachhead as a reenactment of the Normandy invasion gets under way. When they storm the shore, it will not be accompanied by the thunder of enemy artillery, but the clanging of steel drums and on-the-spot radio broadcasting amassed for the Puerto Rican Day celebration, which lays siege to this city with its own barrage of horn-honking, flag-waving nationals.

In the cafeteria of the IBM building, another siege is under way — a quieter, gentler siege. There is a terrifying stillness to the work, laid out on eating tables, that awaits us this Saturday morning, and the transition from corporate cafeteria to graphic morgue is apparent. Our job: to select one hundred for proper interment, while the rest shall be relegated to a mass grave — an ominous cardboard box labeled "out." The jurors, serious and committed, fan out.

By 10:40am, things are already beginning to happen. In ninety short minutes, images of globes have lost their ability to communicate or compel. (We have begun with the annual report category, and already the anesthesia of the mundane has begun its dulling work.) We are numb from shallow-focus globes and soft-focus unispheres afloat in ghastly green photo-ponds that smear these images onto the page. Circles of clouds orbit these montage worlds which sometimes are sporting — yes! — body parts. Hands that cannot move and eyes that cannot see are coughed up from the electronic quicksand of Photoshop. Trying to enliven financials, designers have turned to forensics. It is horrible.

On we go to letterheads, where we tentatively select projects we "like"; some for their inventive ways of getting across some basic information, others for handsome ways of integrating versatility in a program of paper needs. Rudy scours the tables for typography that speaks of exploration. I'm searching for subtlety and clues of humility. Wait! Here's something: the Minneapolis contingent seems to have cornered the "peculiar-fastenings-and-curiously-misappropriated-paper-stock" category, and has done it beautifully. Handsome business cards fit snugly into glassine pockets. Grommets, cleats, staples, springs, nuts and bolts dominate designer's paper needs and self promotions. Later, in the invitations and announcements, I notice something covered in olive corrugated cardboard, bound with raffia and a bit of dried orange peel. Soon, I see a Christmas card recipe booklet that is bound with raffia and a cinnamon stick. I wonder if next year we should have a potpourri category so that this work can be judged fairly on its own merits.

All the while, however, certain pieces are beginning to rise to the surface, just as they are supposed to. Work for Amnesty International[12] that is so simple it haunts. No-nonsense public information on recycling, the science-book-dull annual report for the Marmon Group[13], posters for the Ballet of the Dolls[14] and the Fells Point Theater[15], and satirical Burton Snowboard[16] pieces: these and other projects are beginning to stand out for their clarity or their playfulness, each with some element of surprise within its context or unassailable rightness for its purpose.

12 / SEE PAGE 42, 55

13 / SEE PAGE 75

14 / SEE PAGE 45

15 / SEE PAGE 50

16 / SEE PAGE 71

Surrender

At dinner Laurie and I talk about God. We talk about belief and faith and the difference between them. To summarize, Laurie makes an analogy: "I believe you are a good designer," she suggests, "but I've got to have *faith* in you to ask you to design my identity program." Therefore, we could assume that implicit in faith is an element of surrender.

Most of this book is devoted to the little batch of work that made it "in." There must be something to learn from the majority of work that was passed over. The selection accurately reflects our point of view (that weekend). Doubtless, different days or moods would vary our selection (slightly). One must consider the objective of the 100 Show. There are plenty of venues to show off "great graphic design," but the 100 Show has positioned itself, I believe, around the frontiers of design. My own criteria for judging this show was that great isn't good enough unless there is risk. Beyond this, I was on the outlook for some measure of importance. That is why, among other things you'll notice in this album, there are few stationery programs. Not that they weren't good enough, nor perhaps "great" enough, but hasn't that adjective outgrown the project? A "great" letterhead? Could one be great — at least, that is, when you compare them to a project of the scale and scope of an exhibition, complete with signage and catalog?

Of the entries, I observed that a lot of new, youthful and

exuberant work refuses to commit itself — in language, in type or in image. Designers, it appears, cower behind a camouflage of complexity, taking refuge in confounding rather than clarification. Because of all the hedging, in imagery and typo-technics, work which purports to be a personal vision looks like it was conceived with the multiple views of an unfocused committee! Do we designers who believe in design actually have faith in design?

And what about the *vieux garde*? Firmly entrenched, many dig themselves deeper and deeper into the foxholes of their own reputations. To imitate oneself seems more of a crime than to imitate another — at least the latter takes a little initiative. I wondered whether these designers who seem to have faith in design actually believed in designing!

An equation begins to form in my mind. Risk plus importance can add up to leadership. Ironically though, it is the work that does not surrender that does not lead. Surrendering to a message or a mission became the beacon for the work that excelled, propelling projects to the forefront. When the message rather than the design is the fuel, projects excel.

Victory

Through surrender, I believe, comes victory. For example, contrast the two starkly different books submitted by Callaway Editions. *Native Nations*[17] and *Cyclops*[18] both confront some frontier, and through very different risks excel by design. More specifically: David Carson's overwhelming design conceits in the Albert Watson book bring it to a momentary fashionable forefront, which coincides with Watson's work perfectly. Because of the fleeting nature of these fashion takes, this book earns its fleeting design. The book *should* wallow in the present before the present goes away. Type vogues its way across the pages and we wonder if the pictures are there for the type to play against, or vice-versa, but the inclination of this juror is to award this book — fast — before the impulse goes away. By contrast, *Native Nations* is carefully crafted to preserve a record of a vanished civilization — a second generation whammy. The Edward Curtis photos, like Watson's, seek to document something fleeting.

But because this Native American culture has fled, it deserves the earnest deification this monograph affords it. Here the risk lies in technology, fine reproduction hazarded at press-time, sight unseen, with a civilization at stake. The graphic design of the book pays homage to the images, the typography handsomely recedes. I can't help but wonder: Is Albert Watson jealous?

By contrast to these selections which are mine alone are those where the jurors have respectfully agreed to agree. With Scott Makela's

17 / SEE PAGE 86

18 / SEE PAGE 81

MCAD book[19], the question is less whether the emperor has new clothes, but whether his tailor has gone virtually insane. At the throbbing forefront of techno-macramé, Makela imperils admissions to this art and design college by sending a clear message: "We're so modern we vibrate!" It certainly looks like it works; it's a plugged-in marvel, but the implicit danger is — you guessed it — next year's catalog. Are they still modern if they're still vibrating? How quickly does *l'avant garde* become *le vieux chapeau*?

19 / SEE PAGE 37

The entry which was voted in by consensus and stirred the biggest debate was Margo Johnson's *Hybrid Digital Typefaces*[20]. Undeniably gorgeous in its formal presentation, beautiful studies display classic type with insidious growths that slowly morph and overtake the characters, rendering them illegible. Really! The effect is like a typographic kudzu vine, and we get to watch it slowly and unrelentingly swallow up the alphabet. Bravo Margo! The debate was never whether to include it in the show. The questions that haunt me are about the value of research for its own sake, the value of conquering frontiers of our own making, and the responsibilities of a miner for the thing mined.

20 / SEE PAGE 36

Even outside our IBM cafeteria, on the shores of Lake Michigan, the mock invasion was not proceeding without its glitches. The German gun emplacements were (to the delight of onlookers) firing pretend bullets at a flying formation of Canadian Geese. At sea level there were other problems. Anxious troops were piling out of amphibious landing craft before they engaged the beachhead. David Smith, 29, a dripping wet commercial loan officer from Ft. Wayne, Ind. had just plunged into five feet of chilly water. He could have been referring to the 100 Show judging when he reported, "It was scary. There were spots where some of us couldn't touch."

Fanning the **Flames**

Laurie Haycock Makela

THE BEST PART about writing these notes so long after judging the 100 Show
is that what I remember becomes what was important to me. I remember
that the ACD's curatorial as opposed to democratic approach to the
competition allowed works to be seen that would otherwise never meet
the test of consensus. I remember great shockwaves of work by a couple
of designers, while the rest of the profession seemed to be surreptitious-
ly licking the still-wet excesses off the work of those few. I remember
how, after choosing 100 design works that I enjoyed for one reason or
another, I wanted to scream: "Okay explorers, we're all great. Now let's
go into space!"

Since the judging and now back at the Walker, I've enabled the
design for about 50 print and exhibition graphics, including a magazine,
annual report and catalogue; banners, posters, brochures and flyers,
flyers and more flyers. A big part of my job is knowing my audience and
helping them appreciate the new and different — Walker Art Center is,
after all, a multidisciplinary, contemporary arts museum inspiring local,
national and international communities. Another part of my job is to fan
the experimental fires within the field of design. In the hunt for the
great global village, the Walker design staff is fearlessly moving into the
wilderness of new media, and I'm Tank Girl, puttin' gas in the vehicle.

Audience and multimedia are the subjects of my thinking these
days, so naturally I feel there's something missing in the 100 Show. In the
competition setting, it is impossible to judge the effectiveness of a piece
in terms of audience and that bugs me. By definition, Rudy, Stephen and
I are not the intended audience of any submitted work (nor do we know
who is), so we judge with a fairly limited if not vertiginous point of view.

Multimedia, the design profession's future medium, is as
under-represented in this selection as the idea of audience. The music

and film industry were conspicuously absent; even video submissions were neither new nor different. On the other hand, many designers are still obsessed with designing letterhead (hundreds were submitted), yet only a few are represented here, because it had all been seen, done or overdone.

Our field could use a few new competition categories, such as interactivity and synaesthesia; and ones that expose less product-driven work. Awards for great design lectures, exhibitions, teaching syllabi and results, essays, and design for disabled and minority communities might bestow honor to the "underground" research activities pursued by many of our kind. And could we give the category of letterhead a rest for a few years?

The new work is the workers themselves. Designers such as J. Abbott Miller and Ellen Lupton stand out as leading citizens in our hard-working community. With "Mechanical Brides,"[21] Ellen communicated a wall of thought about culture and design through her exhibition, catalogue, writing and lecture series. The audience bumped into the wall and "got it." J. Abbott Miller designed wonderful books, posters and a landmark magazine called *Dance Ink*[22].

21 / SEE PAGE 56

22 / SEE PAGE 47

The work of ReVerb burst into the room this year and luckily fell easily into the laps of the judges. This fine body of work looks like chain-saw anarchy with moments of deliverence[23]. Lorraine Wild, Somi Kim, Lisa Nugent, Whitney Lowe and Susan Par are the advanced-placement kids who grew muscles and now run the streets, ravishing and revenging design as we know it. I want to call Otis Art Institute's admissions office and ask how it's going. Otis is in the middle of a huge metropolis, often attracting city kids from intensely varied cultures. My guess is that ReVerb's idea of art school marketing is so other, so new and different, that parents and kids may identify with the material for that reason alone. (But how do we know if they do, and when do we ask?)

23 / SEE PAGE 39, 66, 100, 108

The Los Angeles design community punched out of its own great earthquake this year with the most amazing work. With ReVerb, Susan Silton, Rebeca Méndez, the graduate students at CalArts, and many, many other designers, a palpable three-way is going on between Los Angeles' designers, cultural institutions and a diverse audience of more than three million people. Yet the visions are remarkably personal: in particular, Rebeca Méndez's work communicates so much depth that I feel I know her. Her uniquely sensual aesthetic draped itself memorably around promotional material for Art Center College of Design[24] and the Getty Center[25].

24 / SEE PAGE 38, 102
25 / SEE PAGE 92

After seeing almost 2,000 pieces of design in three days, I remember that Rick Valicenti submitted many smart and smart-alecky works[26] fueled by marathon-dance (don't stop 'til you get enough) adrenaline.

26 / SEE PAGE 60, 114, 122, 123

But you won't see the overall spin of his efforts because only a few works were selected for the show. I remember that David Carson also sent many new works that looked just like David Carson works; somehow over time, however, Carson has alienated his colleagues. For better or worse, not much of his work appears here.

I remember that I was proud of Scott Makela's work because everybody thinks everyone does this, this digital thing. But they don't know about massing the unmassable like my astronaut, Scott. They don't all have his alchemist's touch for giving at least one (not every) audience what they want: theatrical delight and controversial fun[27].

27 / SEE PAGE 37, 74

The many literary-like journals submitted to the competition appealed to all of us. Projects where words, images and nerve united in raspy saddle-stitched packages were seen as significant surges in writer/ designer collaborations and desktop publishing. In particular, the weird work from Herron College of Art in Indiana[28] contributes uniquely to the archives of visual storytelling.

28 / SEE PAGE 101

Of course, on-line versions of these same activities will change design's relationship to its audience forever. The sender/receiver diagrams created by early 1980s semioticians will be quickly redrawn. The simultaneity of multimedia will change this culture's thinking from linear to intuitive in unimaginable ways. Information will never travel in a straight line again. Communications in the twenty-first century won't look anything like these nice paper-covered things that go plop on my desk.

After judging the 100 Show, I know there are many inspired and gifted people in our field. Unfortunately, those people are not really working in the twenty-first century yet. That's why I still want to say, "Hey explorers, let's really go out. Let's go, let's go, let's go!"

Wonderful **Wonderment**

Rudy VanderLans

<u>When Rick Poynor invited me</u> to be a juror, I had to think twice. My first thought was why me? What qualifies me to do this? When editing my own magazine, I usually have more questions than answers and I definitely have far more background information on the work published, allowing me an occasional critical angle.

The challenge seemed appealing at the time, however, not least because it offered the opportunity to get a first hand look at the process of judging a design competition. Also, the 100 Show is unique in that it asks the chair, judges and an additional writer to describe the selections and selection process and write accompanying essays, creating an added dimension to the process and outcome.

In writing this essay we were asked to take a critical stance regarding the work we selected. The problem, though, is that there are no real criteria to judge the work by. And, as I quickly found out, it's nearly humanly impossible to go through 1,700 submissions in two days and come up with some 50 selections and accompanying statements. (I'm speaking for myself here; both Laurie and Stephen did a far more capable job in that regard.) You walk into this huge space and face the work, most of which you see for the very first time. You try to take a critical position. You're reminded that the selected work should represent "significant trends," yet the only trend you can detect is an overwhelming variety of graphic design, which is encouraging and which inspired me to round up a selection that would reflect that variety.

But how do you go about picking the "good" from the "bad"? "Problem solving" could be one criteria, but in most cases you don't really know what the problem was. The environment comes to mind when looking at all this paper, but you can't really get a sense of whether the work uses resources in a responsible way. You might be looking at a magazine printed in one color on recycled paper, but if the magazine doesn't have decent distribution it's probably destroying 60% of its print run before people get a chance to see it. None of this is apparent. Cultural or social significance would make any entry worth selecting, but I'm not sure if I'm qualified to make that call on the spot. So without any context, I found myself picking work that I responded to emotionally, which is in itself no small feat except, of course, for those pieces I was already familiar with. I found myself to be quite partial to those entries that I'd seen before, simply because I had more information to judge them by.

I forget now whether we were allowed to pick designer self-promotions. There is a stigma attached to this type of work which I don't understand. As a designer, I find self-promotional work the most difficult to do because there are few parameters. Not taking this work seriously implies that it's only graphic design when an outsider initiates a project, which is nonsense. I picked a few self-promotions without feeling guilty.

Furthermore, for me, this show was marked by two things: the near total absence of magazines and music packaging, two areas where American design pushes boundaries rigorously, and the staggering number of paper promotions and annual reports, two areas where American design splurges. If it wasn't for corporate annual reports and paper company promotions, I wonder if design competitions like this could even exist.

I was disappointed by how few magazines were submitted. Had it been entered, I would have picked *Details* magazine, for instance, because of its intense yet highly readable layouts, use of contemporary, custom-made fonts, and ability to improve what was already a distinctive magazine before it was taken over by Condé Nast a few years ago. I was also disappointed that the new identity for Federal Express hadn't been submitted, because it would have given me an opportunity to pick it for reasons similar to those Neville Brody used in picking last year's Pentagram Prize poster. Federal Express is one of the most forward-looking shipping companies. Their new identity, sadly, places them right back in 1970.

At the end of two days, I find myself sitting behind a table. A tape recorder is spinning and seven or eight people are standing around anxiously waiting for the reason why I selected a piece I was holding. As I flip the pages and try to compose my thoughts, shards of words from the adjoining table where a fellow juror is doing the same filter through: hypertextural, modulation, signifiers, reductivist. The words come without hesitation and enter my train of thought. I can't concentrate. Someone is trying to help me along. "Rudy, I never thought you would pick that one. Tell us why you picked it." Two days of heavy philosophical design discussion and 1,700 entries are racing through my mind, clashing head on with the notion that I might have picked a wrong piece. By picking it, am I contradicting what I said over lunch? I'm nearly starting to hyperventilate and wondering whether I should have told Rick that I didn't think I was qualified.

I know I like the piece, though. And I'm pretty certain it can be considered "good" design. The problem is, I picked it out of sheer wonderment and now have to translate that feeling into cohesive one-liners. I haven't quite made the transition. At the adjoining table words continue to flow. Elaborate, intelligent descriptions that will enhance and help explain the work. How come it's not that clear to me? More doubts creep into my mind. Is the attraction I have for the piece the result of a sly trick by the designer? Am I suckered into believing it's good design simply because the designer knows exactly which strings to pull to get a certain response? But isn't that what design is supposed to do? And who am I to judge this work? As a designer I've always felt particularly unqualified to make objective judgments on issues such as legibility, readability and appropriateness, especially when confronted with "new" work. I can struggle with even the most "legible" designs, simply because I can't stop looking at the type. And isn't appropriateness completely subjective when applied to graphic design?

People are waiting. I need to pull my self-esteem out of the gutter. I try to speak. Discombobulated sentences find their way onto the tiny tape recorder's chrome tape. The little red light is flashing, indicating my words are being recorded. I hold the piece in my hands, and my words are on the tape. There's no connection. It's comforting to know I'll have a chance to edit these comments. I checked out three-quarters through the taping process, feeling dizzy and thoroughly confused.

This was the first design competition I've juried, and in a way it reaffirmed some of my reservations regarding these events. There is simply too much work to evaluate properly. Subsequently, there is a bias to pick work that is familiar. And, as expected, work that I've seen around and believe belongs in a show like this was not entered. What makes the 100 Show more effective than most others, though, is the debates it inspires by asking everybody to sit back for a second, put pen to paper and record their thoughts on the design and selection processes. When reading past 100 Show books, it is the essays and introductions that stand out in my mind, more so than the selected work. The 100 Show, in effect, tells us as much, maybe more, about its chair, contributing writers and jurors, as it does about the entries. For these essays to evolve beyond the discussion of whether design competitions are valuable and what they signify or don't, however, the development of more specific criteria for selecting work might be worth considering.

In closing, I'm left thinking how nice and easy it must have been in the days when Henry Wolf juried design shows. A simple thumbs up or down was all that was expected from a juror. And a consensus was quickly arrived at because everybody knew, apparently without a doubt, what good design was. I'll take sheer wonderment instead, even if it makes me dizzy. And this show provided plenty.

Chicago
Summer
1994

six

The Offices at Copley Place

The I00 +2 show
Consensus

Selections by:
Stephen Doyle

Laurie Haycock Makela

Rudy VanderLans

DESIGNERS
Craig Steen, Sharon Marson

FACULTY DESIGN ADVISOR
George Larou

DESIGN FIRM
Eastern Michigan University Design Area

CLIENT
EMU Student Media

TYPOGRAPHERS
Sharon Marson (Procession)
Craig Steen (Flattop)

PRINTER
Frye

PAPER
Various floor stocks

ENTRANT'S COMMENTS

Cellar Roots was designed by Eastern Michigan University's graduate level graphic design students and showcases student and faculty work. Although the design department considered the past designs successful, some artists and poets were disappointed with how their work was presented. In response, we challenged ourselves to do "fresh," "smart" and "interesting" design from our standpoint, while pleasing our more conservative audience. In an attempt to play on what is considered beautiful and elegant design we created typefaces (Flattop and Procession) based on the proportions of Bodoni. We also looked at fine books from medieval manuscripts through the arts and crafts period, including research on the golden mean and nuances found in the letterpress. We tried to maintain the elegance found in these designs while tucking in some inside jokes and poking fun at the styles we researched as well as our past critics.

JURORS' COMMENTS

This is an oddity, a real curio. I like how old fashioned it is. I like the way it keeps referring to itself. It's really fun to read. I don't care for the cover and I could do without the vellum. That aside, there's nice restraint and joy in this little exploration. **S.D.**

The classical type is surrounded by very peculiar ornamentation. Each page is designed differently, creating an intricate and elegantly fractured look. **L.H.M.**

It's the balance between familiarity and experimentation that holds my attention. Although I can't assume to know the precise, scientific level of its legibility, this design shows me that an idiosyncratic, customized font does not necessarily make reading difficult. In fact, it adds character and individualism to the project. **R.V.D.L.**

DESIGNER
Chris Froeter

WRITER
Margaret Benson

DESIGN DIRECTOR
Ted Stoik

PHOTOGRAPHER
Tony Armour

DESIGN FIRM
VSA Partners, Inc.

CLIENT
Chicago Volunteer Legal Services

TYPOGRAPHER
Chris Froeter

PRINTER/SEPARATOR
HM Graphics

PAPER
Mohawk Superfine

ENTRANT'S COMMENTS

Chicago Volunteer Legal Services is a not-for-profit organization made up of lawyers working on a volunteer basis to protect the rights of people who could not otherwise afford legal services. This book celebrates the selfless work of these volunteers. The case studies document the extreme need for legal services found in the financially poor but spiritually rich neighborhoods of Chicago. The legal work is rendered in an authentic manner — solving the clients' problem in their culturally diverse neighborhoods, in their own languages. The design reflects that authenticity.

JUSTICE SHOULD KNOW
NO BOUNDARIES.

OUR ACTION IS DRIVEN
BY OUR FAITH IN
THE SYSTEM.

JURORS' COMMENTS

It's colorful, it's frank, it's not fussy. It's a straightforward presentation. The cover says something about what it is. **S.D.**

This piece is appropriate and simple, and the case studies add integrity. **L.H.M**

These lawyers are obviously not going to charge you $175 per hour, and that comes across very effectively in this design. **R.V.D.L.**

**Confetti Quarterly
Reports on Stock**

DESIGNERS
Steven Tolleson, Jennifer Sterling

ART DIRECTORS
Steven Tolleson, Jennifer Sterling

WRITER
Lindsay Beaman

PHOTOGRAPHER
John Casado

DESIGN FIRM
Tolleson Design

CLIENT
Fox River Paper Company

PRINTER/SEPARATOR
Lithographix Inc.

PAPER
Fox River Confetti

ENTRANT'S COMMENTS

These quarterly reports were designed to promote Confetti by Fox River Paper Company in the annual report market. The books are reminiscent in size of quarterly reports issued to shareholders. Information contained in each of the four books is accessible in two forms. The first is the production performance of Confetti and the various printing techniques that have been applied in the design process. Each of the books has a title page that incorporates letterpress, engraving, debossing or thermography. The inside covers simulate a financial make-ready sheet while technically showing how fluorescent, four color, metallic, transparent, match and opaque inks perform on Confetti. The second level contains technical information on annual report terms, production techniques and competition deadlines valuable to the annual report designer. Each of these relates photographically to the message contained in each book.

JURORS' COMMENTS

They're delightful. They've got great imagery. They show off the paper well and contain understandable **information that is actually useful to know.** A treat. Something you want to hang on to. **S.D.**

The designer pays attention to details with great results. The images are unusual and informative. **L.H.M.**

I picked this for the same reason I picked their Radius Annual Report. **R.V.D.L.**

Eye Q

Product Identity

DESIGNER
Eric Handel

ILLUSTRATOR
John Grotting

DESIGN FIRM
LMNOP

CLIENT
New Video Corporation

ENTRANT'S COMMENTS

The product was the first video application for the Macintosh, so my client wanted an identity that was "in your face." The most difficult aspect of the job was creating the product name. We began the process heading in a "new age" direction with Vision Quest, which finally translated into Eye Q, a name open to more interpretation. This was further amplified by creating a bold, futuristic/techno-pop character using 3D animation software.

JURORS' COMMENTS

I like its sense of humor. **S.D.**

One question: can such a smart visual idea work as well in black and white? **L.H.M.**

I hope the eye rotates within the Q and occasionally winks at you when it's used in a video. **R.V.D.L.**

DESIGNER
Jennifer E. Moody

WRITER
Jennifer E. Moody

CLIENT
California Institute of the Arts

SILKSCREEN PRINTING
Jennifer E. Moody

PAPER
Limogé

ENTRANT'S COMMENTS

The curators of the furniture show had two concerns: that with all the many "postered" events going on at that time, the announcement for their show should stand out in some way, and that all the artists who had committed to the show finish their pieces in time. The chair was "life size," and the posters were hung accordingly. (Get it?) The names of everyone who had committed were included on the poster as incentive to finish their work on time. (Some smarty-pants came up with a rubber stamp and as people "flaked" they were branded as a "QUITTER.")

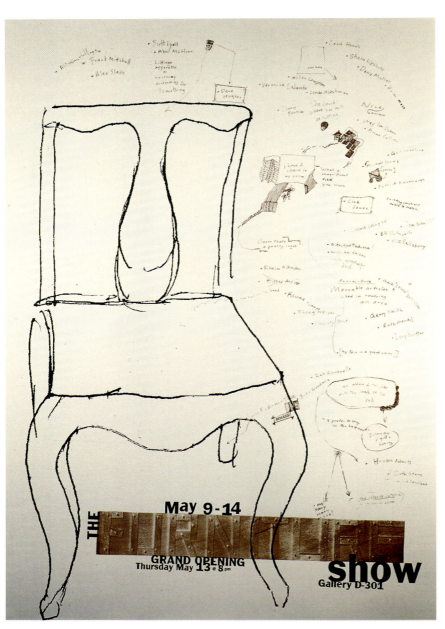

JURORS' COMMENTS

I like the offhandedness of this poster. The giant fax sketch has a softness and familiarity about it that is appealing. The doodles imply that if you go to the show you're going to have fun because they're actually going to let you in on the process of the design of the furniture in the show. **S.D.**

The drawings tell a story and the scale of the poster is very expressive. **L.H.M.**

The process of design, the making of prototypes and the craft and production of furniture are all effectively visualized in this poster. Presenting this kind of information in such a loose way, without an obvious grid, while remaining structured and solidly balanced is not easy. The image bristles with energy but still gets the basic information across effectively. **R.V.D.L.**

DESIGNERS
Steve Pattee, Kelly Stiles, Cindy Poulton

WRITER
Mike Condon

DESIGN FIRM
Pattee Design

CLIENT
Metro Waste Authority

PRINTER
Seward Graphics

PAPER
French Dur-o-tone, Champion Benefit

ENTRANT'S COMMENTS

The objective was to create a comprehensive guide to waste management for business in general. The piece is actually eight 4-page brochures bound into the cover so specific information could be targeted and waste could be avoided. This is the proverbial 10 lbs. in a 5 lb. bucket project.

JURORS' COMMENTS

It looks to me like something that people would actually read. Everything's capsulized. There's some real information here. It's presented in a straightforward, fun, ugly newsletter manner, which seems wildly appropriate. People are going to respond to it because it looks so familiar in a positive way. There's something "free kittens, tear off the phone number" about this approach. **S.D.**

The newspaper vernacular turns the content into ads or articles. As a result the concepts are accessible. **L.H.M.**

Finally, an annual report I dare touch with my bare hands and that I don't have to slant this way and that in order to see through the glare of super slick coated paper. **R.V.D.L.**

DESIGNER
Margo Johnson

TYPE DESIGNS
Margo Johnson

ENTRANT'S COMMENTS

To challenge the tradition of hand-rendered type with brush and plaka, I began to experiment using technology as a design process. I applied mathematical variables to an existing typeface. The results produced random and unexpected letterforms. I devised a system using a numerical matrix to apply to three typefaces: serif, sans serif and script. Three volumes of 20 new fonts were generated, each named and ordered according to the matrix. I designed a traditional type specimen book with an introduction and diagrams which showcase the 60 typefaces.

JURORS' COMMENTS

There is something remarkably compelling and even reassuring about this marvelous book of type gone awry. I conjure up someone in a tower with a computer. The effort has got to be applauded, even if I'm not sure what to make of the result. There's something vaguely Rumplestiltskinian about this exercise, spinning all that type into obliteration, and I detect some black humor in this very formal presentation. **S.D.**

If 50% of aesthetics is completion, then the aesthetics of this study are very satisfying. This is one of my favorite pieces in the show, because of its poker-faced humor and unbridled experimentation. For an unmanageable study in typographic abandon, the research and development is beautifully presented. **L.H.M.**

This is one of my favorite pieces in the entire show. It's funny, too, because after seeing the cover, the last thing you expect is this incredible, complete abandonment of the tradition of standards in type design. The presentation of the research and development is done well, and this type of material is not easy to organize and present coherently. **R.V.D.L.**

DESIGNER
P. Scott Makela

VIDEO
Rik Sferra, Alex Tylevich, P. Scott Makela

DESIGN FIRM
Words+Pictures

CLIENT
Minneapolis College of Art and Design

PRINTER
Bolger Publications

ENTRANT'S COMMENTS

Our concept here had a few positive restrictions.
First, have a slightly lower "signal to noise" ratio than
our 1991-93 catalog. (The president's request!) Second,
use high 8mm videography as the main source of
photography. Finally, use bolder and more legible text
(for the nervous Minnesota rural fathers and mothers).
Further explorations into the architecture of the
language (the virtual keyframes like "WHAT IT IS/WHO
WE ARE/AND WHY" under DEFINE) are fully read after
continued viewings.

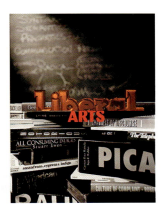

JURORS' COMMENTS

I've hated this when I've seen it reproduced. A lot of the things that we've chosen have an intrinsic glory in person.
I had no idea how much power, impact and exuberance this thing contained with all its technicolor imagery and
wildly screaming type. It's really great fun. **S.D.**

This is a masterful project where **the designer plays magician and band leader,**
waking his audience up with masterful tricks, costumes and sheer volume. **L.H.M.**

Some of the typefaces and typography in this catalog can be considered **quite hideous,** but it's all
presented in such a brazen way, without apologies, always challenging or nearly demanding you to read. And where
it really counts, most of the information is perfectly accessible. I hope MCAD can live up to the excitement offered
in this catalog. **R.V.D.L.**

**OBJECTS: Sixteen
L.A. Sculptors**

Designer
Darin Beaman, Rebeca Méndez

Writers
The curators and artists

Design Firm
ACCD Design Office

Client
Art Center College of Design

Printer/Separator
Typecraft Inc.

Paper
Matrix Dull

Entrant's Comments

The form of this exhibition catalog addresses the notion of the book as object. By exposing the binding threads and cheese cloth we emphasize their materiality as part of a book's production process. Stripping the book of its hard cover and using cover stock for text pages continues the strategy of "defamiliarizing" the book. The ways in which these four elements are combined create a subtle category confusion between book and object. By contrast the catalog's content, photography and text focus on the artists and their processes rather than their finished objects.

Jurors' Comments

The fringe on the binding makes you conscious of the book as an object, reinforcing the thing. It's a design delight on the inside, the typography as well as the photographs, the arrangement and the disarrangement. I admire the power of how the pages are activated. I love the folios in the middle of the page. I could never get away with that. It's got a lot of exquisite and smart detailing. **S.D.**

This is not your typical art catalog. Through the use of various devices the designer made the book itself an object — not accidentally, of course, as the show is called "Objects." **L.H.M.**

Although there's only one color used throughout this catalog, the overall result is far more colorful, dynamic and engaging than most efforts by designers using six colors and special effects. Rebeca's work continues to impress me no end. **R.V.D.L.**

DESIGNER
Lisa Nugent

WRITERS
Various

PHOTOGRAPHER
Dennis Keeley

DESIGN FIRM
ReVerb, Los Angeles

CLIENT
Otis College of Art and Design

TYPOGRAPHER
Lisa Nugent, Whitney Lowe, Somi Kim

PRINTER/SEPARATOR
Frye & Smith

PAPER
Dull coat web, Mohawk Recycled,
Champion Carnival

ENTRANT'S COMMENTS

This Otis catalog is structured around the idea of setting things in motion as it portrays the various environments on campus which serve as testing grounds for interesting work. It attempts to visualize the creative atmosphere while highlighting the high level of work that is produced each year. Throughout the text are gate folds which provide unexpected visual juxtapositions to reinforce the idea of open inquiry and opportunity. A recruitment catalog is usually the first impression of a college that potential students receive with the express purpose of generating additional inquiry into the college's programs. The catalog must therefore provide a visual sense of the college's personality and educational philosophy as well as detailed and technical information in the form of text.

JURORS' COMMENTS

This not my taste at all, honestly. But what's great about it is that it's appropriate to its audience and its market. It reeks of enthusiasm. If I were 16 or 17, it would pique my interest about this place because there's so much cacophony about the presentation. It's a joyous celebration of this school. What it lacks in legibility is compensated for by energy and curiosity, which is the whole objective of a catalog like this. **S.D.**

A gregarious flair for bulbous shapes, ganked (sic) type, and geastly (sic) color distinguishes this piece. **L.H.M.**

Simply way cool. **R.V.D.L.**

Radius Inc.

1992 Annual Report

DESIGNERS
Steven Tolleson, Mark Winn

WRITER
Lindsay Beaman

PHOTOGRAPHY
Coll Photography

DESIGN FIRM
Tolleson Design

CLIENT
Radius Inc.

PRINTER/SEPARATOR
Pacific Lithograph

PAPER
Karma

ENTRANT'S COMMENTS

Although Radius is known primarily as a display and accelerator board company, the goal of this annual report was to underscore its progress in providing complete graphic systems solutions for the electronic color publishing and desktop video markets. Radius's mission and strategies are presented in Q&A format on a black background, interspersed with customer perspectives on the impact Radius products have had on their business.

JURORS' COMMENTS

There's a maniacal attention to detail. The stuff down the edge of the page is really cool, and it looks really great. He's letting the page masquerade as a video screen. The photographs, however, are vague and boring. **S.D.**

Sublime quality. **L.H.M.**

Perhaps as a reaction to my interest in anti-mastery, at times I hunger for hyper-mastery.

The care put into the typographic detail and the overall richness of the typography are the hallmarks of most of Tolleson's designs. There's a perfect balance between emotion and restraint, stylishness and functionality, which works well within the realm of annual reports. I have never seen a piece Tolleson has designed that looks rushed or tired. To me, he is one of the great modern craftsman designers. **R.V.D.L.**

The Raynes Rail

DESIGNER/INVENTOR
Coco Raynes

DESIGNERS
Karen LeDuc, Matt Kanaracus

PHOTOGRAPHER
Bill Miles

SPONSOR
The Massachusetts Eye and Ear Infirmary

MANUFACTURERS
Milgo, New England Plastics

ENTRANT'S COMMENTS

The Raynes Rail has been designed to allow visually impaired visitors to travel independently throughout unknown buildings and open spaces. The handrail system has Braille messages on its inner face and audio information at strategic locations of offices, ramps, stairs and elevators. The push button audio units have multilingual applications and can be used by the public at large, making the rail a universal design. The Raynes Rail exceeds the requirements outlined in Title III of the Americans with Disabilities Act (ADA) of 1992. The ADA mandated that all doors within public buildings be identified with Braille. There was no provision, however, for any link between the entrance of a building to a door sign. Our design makes up for this deficiency.

JURORS' COMMENTS

I personally admire designers who do this kind of work. You're not going to get much visibility doing this. It's not an annual report or a big poster; it's very quiet, but so unbelievably important. **S.D.**

This is problem solving of a high order, and effectively broadens our interpretation of visual communication. While not visual itself, braille tucked in the railing helps the visitor "see." **L.H.M.**

In an area where visual hype often reigns, this is a particularly striking design. One has to admire designers who do this kind of work. **R.V.D.L.**

DESIGNERS
Hal Wolverton, Alicia Johnson

WRITERS
Alicia Johnson, Hal Wolverton

DESIGN FIRM
Johnson & Wolverton

CLIENT
Amnesty International USA

PRINTER/ FILM
Irwin-Hodson Company

PAPER
Evergreen Matte

ENTRANT'S COMMENTS

This project sought to raise awareness, develop membership and promote activism for the youth/student program of Amnesty International. Our approach was to appeal to the energy, idealism and rebelliousness of this audience by inviting them to be a "terrorist" for the good of human rights.

SPREAD
"RUMORS"

PROPAGATE
"LIES"

PUBLISH
"SUBVERSIVE"
LITERATURE

BE A
"TERRORIST"

INCITE
HOPE

JURORS' COMMENTS

It's tasteful. The type and the photographic softness gives it an underground character. The best thing about it is that it's succinct. Usually, organizations like this go on with reams of copy paper and can't get you to read it. This hits their nail on the head. **S.D.**

A quiet, confident, underground approach. **L.H.M.**

This reeks of the underground. It has the **forbidden and secretive** feel, like a Russian "samizdat" publication, of something that has been handed down from person to person, making it all the more desirable to read. **R.V.D.L.**

The 1OO[+2] show
Two Jurors

Stephen Doyle

+

Laurie Haycock Makela

Laurie Haycock Makela

+

Rudy VanderLans

Rudy VanderLans

+

Stephen Doyle

DESIGNERS
Eric Altenburger, Elizabeth Barrett, Richard Bates,
Charlie Becker, Thomas Bricker, John Codling,
Allie Cohen, Darren Crawforth, Jean Cronin,
Frank Gargiulo, Jamie Goldberg, Allen Hori,
Lynn Kowalewski, Sung Lee-Crawforth,
Donald May, Melanie Nissen, Michelle Piza,
Jennifer Roddie, Cozbi Sanchez-Cabrera,
Laura Shane, David Statman, Valerie Wagner

DESIGN FIRM/CLIENT
Atlantic Records Art Dept.

PRINTER
Time Warner Print Shop

SEPARATOR
Cardinal Communications

PAPER
Vintage Velvet

ENTRANT'S COMMENTS

Articulating a sense of individuality in word, image and deed in the corporate environment is paramount for this creative department. The creation of an energized studio environment with art directors and designers who capitalize on their autonomy and whose processes are free from hierarchical weight is communicated through these idiosyncratic business cards. The press sheet of cards reflects the studio's confidence in the strengths of its individual members as well as the department's profile as a creative force within the company.

JURORS' COMMENTS

This is good, healthy fun. What the heck? This is the way a business card should look if you work at Atlantic. They're like a stack of CDs, only smaller and cheaper. Besides, you could always call information if you needed their phone number, right? **S.D.**

I usually only like business cards that stick to the facts, but these are okay because they've got a house groove going. Loose and funky. **L.H.M.**

DESIGNER
Matt Eller

WRITER
Myron Johnson

PHOTOGRAPHER
Mike Crouser

CLIENT
Ballet of the Dolls

TYPOGRAPHER
Matt Eller

ENTRANT'S COMMENTS

This street poster for Ballet of the Dolls is a stark promotion for a dance company known for its classical-meets-disco sensibility. I like to think that the two huge (size matters) letterforms imply a cross-pollinating of sexual preference.

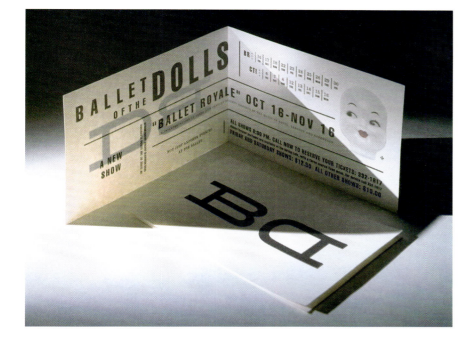

JURORS' COMMENTS

I like this poster for its curious size. It's spanking fresh. The type is clean. It's certainly restrained. There's just one spot of second color, and it does its job. **S.D.**

The poster is like a giant ticket. The designer makes a few eerily simple moves to create a strangely (bi)sexual innuendo with the letterforms BD. Can't miss that from the street. **L.H.M.**

DESIGNERS
Dana Arnett, Curt Schreiber

WRITERS
Anita Liskey, Michael Oakes

PHOTOGRAPHER
François Robert

DESIGN FIRM
VSA Partners, Inc.

CLIENT
Chicago Board of Trade

TYPOGRAPHER
Curt Schreiber

PRINTER/SEPARATOR
The Hennegan Company

PAPER
Gilbert Cotton, Neutech

open

bid

offer

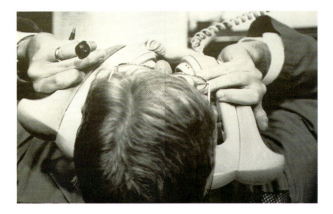

ENTRANT'S COMMENTS

This annual report is about a trading institution's record breaking year. The reader is paced through a day in the life of a trader by documenting the significant moments of the trading experience. Explosive graphics and editorial photography dominate the book to tell the story. A limited color palette was chosen to keep the focus on the content. A thin writing stock for body and cover allows for plenty of "see through" for dynamic entrances and exits from each spread of the book.

JURORS' COMMENTS

I'm impressed by the typographic narrative. You hear the bell. You sense the cacophony, see the motion. The type and the photography are narrative. You feel like you're experiencing it. It's exciting! It really brings it to life. Look at how bold and simple those two colors are on the nice, thin, uncoated paper; it's got all the right antique production values that so many are striving to achieve. Ding ding! **S.D.**

Thinking of the Board of Trade, I picture rows of teeny numbers. The friendly scale of this piece makes the teeny numbers comprehensible, funny and even exciting. It uses childlike ways of expressing grownup ideas. **L.H.M.**

Dance Ink

DESIGNER
J. Abbott Miller

EDITOR
Lise Friedman

PHOTOGRAPHERS
Joanne Savio, Josef Astor and others

DESIGN FIRM
Design Writing Research

PUBLISHER
Dance Ink, Patricia Tarr

TYPOGRAPHER
J. Abbott Miller

PRINTER
The Studley Press

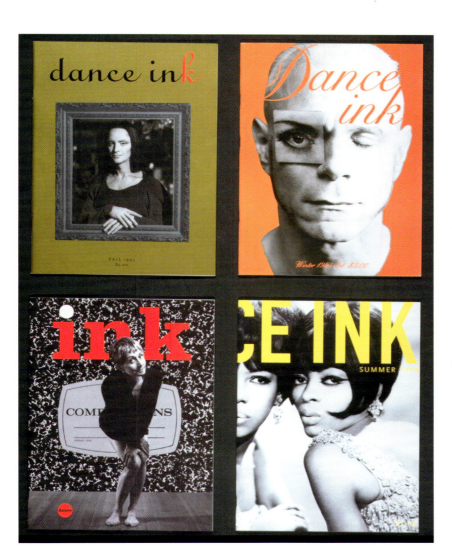

ENTRANT'S COMMENTS

This quarterly not-for-profit magazine features thoughtful writing and photography about classical and avant garde forms of dance, performance and the visual arts. The design responds to both the literary tenor of the essays and the visual intensity of the photography. Typography is the common denominator between the scholarly and populist impulses that define the scope of the magazine's interests. The design of the magazine has evolved from issue to issue, retaining a consistent setting for body copy while varying display fonts, sometimes featuring two or three experimental fonts in each issue. The restriction to three-color printing was originally an economic decision, but the use of duotone printing has since become an important part of the magazine's aesthetic. The design of the magazine has evolved by virtue of the support and trust of the magazine's publisher and editor.

JURORS' COMMENTS

Dance Ink is a welcome exception to the class of small-circulation magazine wanna-bes that echo and imitate their large-circulation forebears. It is confident, nonchalant and has tons of personality. The beautiful detailing comes across as offhand, and the whole magazine exudes fluidity from front to back. I'm envious. **S.D.**

The design of this magazine is evolving before our eyes. The logo changes on every cover, the whole format flexes, and the type is extremely sensitive to content. **L.H.M.**

Disclosure

Cover and Binding

DESIGNER
Chip Kidd

WRITER
Michael Crichton

DESIGN FIRM
Kidd

PUBLISHER
Knopf

TYPOGRAPHER
JCH

PRINTER
Coral Graphics

PAPER
Varivue Vellum

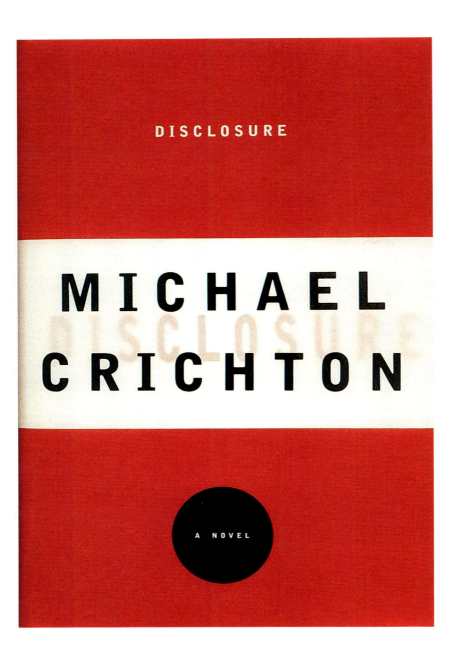

ENTRANT'S COMMENTS

If less is more, then it doesn't get much more than this.
The simplicity is deceptive, however: the long trail
of acetate, cardboard, neon ink, eye balls, ripped shirts
and digitized puckered lips (all generated by myself,
I'll admit) that lead to this design makes for a
heart-breaking and profoundly dull story.
To his credit, all the author ultimately wanted was
a cover treatment that played on the book's title.
Additional kudos to the powers that be for not making
me typeset the words "Jurassic" or "Park" in
connection with this project.

JURORS' COMMENTS

Fast and simple. There's nice tactility to it, which makes it curious on the shelf. The plastic wrapper is a good
chaser to "A Secret History." What's next, Chip? **S.D.**

This designer knows that when you don't know what to do, make it red. It really works. Why does every Kidd book
jacket catch my eye? **L.H.M.**

DESIGNER
Irma Boom

DESIGN FIRM
Irma Boom

CLIENT
KPN, Royal PTT Netherland

TYPOGRAPHER
Irma Boom

PRINTER/SEPARATOR
Joh. Enschede

ENTRANT'S COMMENTS

The butterfly is one of the ten most desirable images for a postage stamp. Thus a postage stamp featuring Dutch diurnal butterflies should have been an easy design assignment, if the dreaded cliché didn't lie in wait. The theme for the issue, nature and environment, threw another light on the matter. Butterflies are important ecological indicators; of the 75 species of diurnal butterflies once found in the Netherlands, fifteen are extinct and fourteen more are threatened. By picturing the butterflies only in part, attention is shifted from the decorative to the indicative. The text in the colored bars underscores the message.

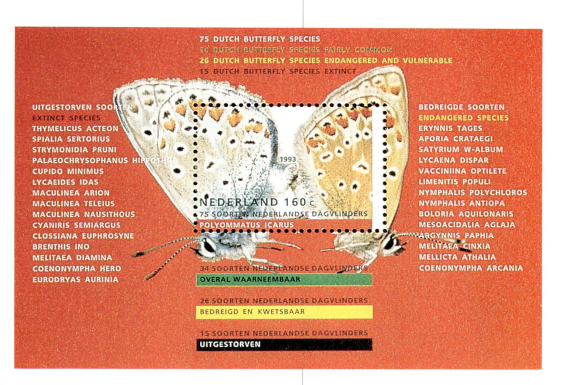

JURORS' COMMENTS

How could you not like stamps of butterflies, especially when they're designed by Irma Boom? They're gorgeous little things. The butterfly on an envelope is a nice metaphor, too, fluttering off to the addressee. S.D.

The designer understands scale, visual pleasure, and the potential of the stamp to carry bits of information about, in this case, the non-controversial butterfly. L.H.M.

DESIGNERS/PRINTERS
**Paul Sahre,
David Plunkert,
Joe Parisi**

CLIENT
Fells Point Corner Theatre

ENTRANT'S COMMENTS

**Freebie silkscreen posters for a community
theater in Baltimore.**

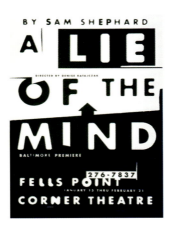

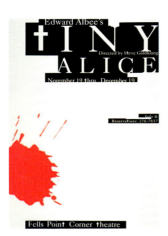
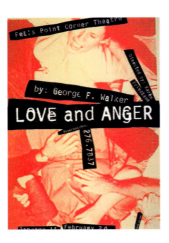

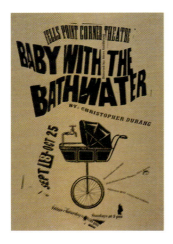

JURORS' COMMENTS

The consistency of the size and the restricted palattes add to the identity of the theater, even though the imagery
and typography are diverse. Consistent inconsistency: my kind of thing! Intriguing without being pushy. **S.D.**

Quick and dirty representations of theatrical productions. Versatile. Street. **L.H.M.**

DESIGNER
Anita Meyer

WRITER/CURATOR
Anne-Marie Logan

EXHIBITION COORDINATOR
Judith Hoos Fox

PRODUCTION COORDINATOR
Susan McNally

DESIGN FIRM
plus design inc.

CLIENT
Davis Museum and Cultural Center

TYPOGRAPHER
Moveable Type Inc.

PRINTER/SEPARATOR
Snoeck-Ducaju + Zoon

PAPER
Mellotex Cartridge, archival binder's boards

ENTRANT'S COMMENTS

Inspired by late 19th- and early 20th-century
drawing books and folios, this exhibition catalog
provides a reinterpretation of these early publications.
The glorified spine, uncovered bookbinder's board
and debossed corners allude to historical books and
folios while rethinking tradition. The book is bound
to open flat which facilitates viewing the images.
The calendared uncoated stock suggests the papers
on which the drawings were originally executed.
The typography is based on historical conventions
which have been rethought, as the analyses of the
drawings offer new interpretations.

JURORS' COMMENTS

Juxtaposing the modern mode of this book with the old Flemish drawings makes this thing ignite. The color of the
cardboard cover jives with the color of the drawings, and the orange adds just the right spark. And look at those
folios! The pages of type are like beautiful calm lakes. Don't you just want to
jump in? **S.D.**

The little bit of orange on the spine lets the reader know that this book was made in 1994 and not the 19th century.
Careful, exquisitely managed typography and beautiful scale shifts make this book special. **L.H.M.**

Foamex Capabilities

Brochure

DESIGNERS
Peter Harrison, Susan Hochbaum,
Kevin Lauterbach

WRITER
Bruce Duffy

PHOTOGRAPHERS
Kenji Toma, John Madere

DESIGN FIRM
Pentagram

CLIENT
Foamex International

PRINTER
Sandy Alexander

PAPER
Potlatch Eloquence

ENTRANT'S COMMENTS

Foamex is the largest marketer and manufacturer of
flexible polyurethane foam and foam products in North
America. Pentagram designed a capabilities brochure
to attract potential investors to this newly public
company. Vivid graphics and photography enliven
management and financial statements and reflect
Foamex's aggressive corporate character and growth
strategy. The brochure was bound with covers made of
reticulated foam to articulate the company's identity
and present its product in an unusual, direct way.

JURORS' COMMENTS

One big hurrah for tactility, and three cheers for foam! Isn't every designer jealous of Peter
Harrison et al for getting to design a brochure for a company that manufactures thin foam that begs to be used on
the cover? The blow-up photo is the next nice surprise, and even though the rest of the photographs are sensory-
challenged, the book is bright, bold and punchy. S.D.

Its obvious materiality appeals to me. It successfully foregrounds an otherwise functional, behind-
the-scenes product. L.H.M.

Geoffrey Beene Unbound

Exhibit, Catalog and Poster

DESIGNER
J. Abbott Miller

DESIGN FIRM
Design Writing Research

CLIENT
Geoffrey Beene and The Museum of the Fashion
Institute of Technology

TYPOGRAPHER
J. Abbott Miller

FABRICATORS
F.I.T. Crew

ARCHITECTURAL CONSULTANT
Alex Manuele

VIDEO CONSULTANT
Judith Barry

PRINTER
The Studley Press

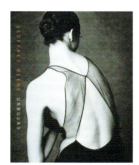
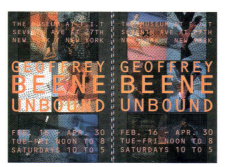

ENTRANT'S COMMENTS

A major 30-year retrospective of clothing designer Geoffrey Beene presented the opportunity to coordinate the design of the exhibition, book and promotional graphics. The focal point of the exhibit was four massive criss-crossing stairways flanking a gauzy apparition of women appearing to glide back and forth through space on three different scrims. The walls of the exhibit played off of Beene's gestures of black and white stripes, polka dots and accents of strong color, but at a massive environmental scale. The crisp sans serif fonts were carried over to the book. The dense four color photography is related to the richness of textiles by the "pinking shears" edge with which the book is trimmed. The posters, wheat-pasted in public locations and also used in the exhibit as a wall covering, were produced by silkscreening orange text over the printers make-ready sheets for the book.

JURORS' COMMENTS

So many people are trying to do something with the press sheet. Here that idea is used to sheer advantage. It's a beautiful, ethereal, veiling way to project an imagine for a Geoffrey Beene show. It's so right. There's a wonderful semi-gloss latex economy to this exhibit. What appeals to me about this entire package is that it is so terribly appropriate to the exhibition: the wall, the photograph mountings, the giant arrow directing you down the stairs. **S.D.**

Transforming a book press sheet into a poster by layering the lace and type is smart, constructive and beautiful. **L.H.M.**

Harley-Davidson, Inc.

1993 Annual Report

DESIGNERS
Dana Arnett, Curt Schreiber

WRITER
Ken Schmidt

ILLUSTRATOR
John Youssi

PHOTOGRAPHER
James Schrepf

DESIGN FIRM
VSA Partners, Inc.

CLIENT
Harley-Davidson, Inc.

TYPOGRAPHER
VSA Partners, Inc.

PRINTER/SEPARATOR
George Rice and Sons

PAPER
Mead Escanaba Enamel, Moistrite Matte

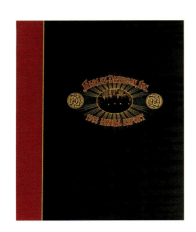

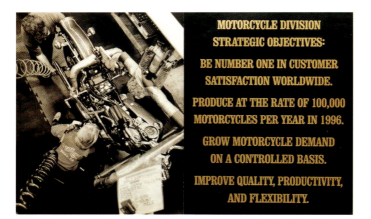

MOTORCYCLE DIVISION
STRATEGIC OBJECTIVES:
BE NUMBER ONE IN CUSTOMER
SATISFACTION WORLDWIDE.
PRODUCE AT THE RATE OF 100,000
MOTORCYCLES PER YEAR IN 1996.
GROW MOTORCYCLE DEMAND
ON A CONTROLLED BASIS.
IMPROVE QUALITY, PRODUCTIVITY,
AND FLEXIBILITY.

ENTRANT'S COMMENTS

In 1993 Harley-Davidson, Inc. saluted the "Family of Harley-Davidson." This annual report features photography, color and type that work to create a visual language coherent to the personality of the corporation, its people and its products. A special commemorative poster featuring the events of the 90th anniversary further promoted and commemorated the anniversary year.

JURORS' COMMENTS

This book seems to rumble at the same time that it sports lots of little, minute detailing. But the whole thing has a massiveness and a black leatherness that charges it. I'm constantly amazed how Dana Arnett can make new vernacular references work. This looks like Time magazine in 1964, but there's something that's really fresh and knowingly appropriate about it. Look at the blackness of the charts. They really do their job. Burning rubber! **S.D.**

The big, solid type is like the company's products: cool. **L.H.M.**

Human Rights Abuse

Poster

DESIGNERS
Hal Wolverton, Alicia Johnson, Adam McIsaac,
Kat Saito, Jerome Schiller

WRITER
Alicia Johnson

PHOTOGRAPHER
Rafael Astorga

DESIGN FIRM
Johnson & Wolverton

CLIENT
Amnesty International USA

FILM/PRINTER
Irwin-Hodson Company

PAPER
Simpson Evergreen Matte

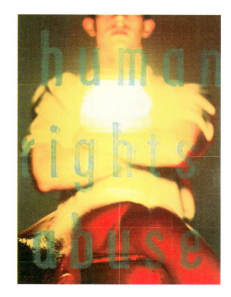

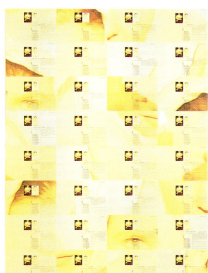
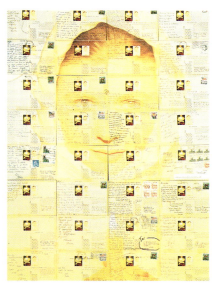

ENTRANT'S COMMENTS

Our purpose was to provide students with information about Amnesty International and an action for their first meeting. Our approach was to create a ritual to express the work of AI. Tearing apart the front side, "Human Rights Abuse" is a symbol of the work Amnesty International does worldwide. Sending out the postcards is a tangible action teaching the students about the work of AI (primarily letter-writing). Recomposed, "hope" is a symbol of the spirit generated by the work of AI. At the end of the academic year, recomposed posters traveled throughout the U.S. to high school and university campuses as a tribute to a year of hard work, as a reminder of the work yet to be done, and as a call for new memberships.

JURORS' COMMENTS

There's a power and directness to this piece. Best are the little bits of information on the postcards describing individually Amnesty International's commitment, the state of the world, and what they're fighting about. I like the interactive nature of it, that you tear it up and send it out. It's a poetic gesture of participation and hope. **S.D.**

While it may be too pretty for its subject, this poster uses its aesthetic force to seduce the viewer into action.
L.H.M.

EXHIBITION DESIGNERS
Ellen Lupton, Laurene Leon, Constantin Boym

GRAPHIC DESIGNERS
Ellen Lupton, Hall Smyth, J. Abbott Miller

DESIGN FIRMS
**Cooper-Hewitt,
National Design Museum,
Boym Studio**

CLIENT
Cooper-Hewitt, National Museum of Design

PRINTER
The Studley Press

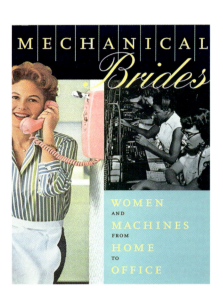

ENTRANT'S COMMENTS

This exhibition and publication linked artifacts of industrial design, including typewriters, telephones, washing machines and electric irons, with their representation in various media in order to show how these objects have served as symbols and instruments of "women's work" in the 20th century. The curatorial and design teams aimed to give a vivid, accessible form to the feminist literature on women and design by linking three-dimensional objects with media images and the stories of actual users. For example, the Telephone Wall presented back-lit images from movies and advertising of women rapturously engaged with their telephones. Mounted on the wall are phones which featured the recorded voices of working women, including telephone operators, a receptionist, and Lily Tomlin's fictional character Ernestine.

JURORS' COMMENTS

Until this show pointed it out, who would've thought that the seemingly benign act of designing a telephone was an act fraught with sexual innuendo? This show focuses on design as sociology, throwing a whole new light on what we do, and making its importance reach far beyond its scope. Look. There are even messages hanging on the laundry line. Far from being bookish or catalog-y, the book relishes its magazine antecedents. It's jam-packed with images of good old American "progress," yet never descends into camp. But it's the entire concept of this show that deserves our applause. What an undertaking! **S.D.**

Lupton is doing remarkable curatorial work by showing design in a social and cultural context. In this case, she is looking at gender in industrial design. I deeply respect the entire effort. This book is a labor of research, humor and love, packed into too few pages. **L.H.M.**

DESIGNERS
Chip Kidd, Barbara de Wilde

WRITER
Dennis Donoghue

DESIGN FIRM
Kidd & de Wilde

CLIENT
Knopf

TYPOGRAPHER
JCH

PRINTER
Coral Graphics

PAPER
Crispy Papel

ENTRANT'S COMMENTS

We'd be lying if we said that we actually understood this book, not that we doubt its apparent brilliance and keen presence of mind for a second. The sad ugly truth is that we already tried this approach on a book about logic, only to be laughed at and quickly dismissed. Never ones to invent something new when the past is plunderable, we presented the design when the time and subject were right.

JURORS' COMMENTS

I like the visual analogy of different kinds of rules as a metaphor for essays on literature and theory. How can we resist? **S.D.**

Modern is such an old word. Using the two words — old and modern — together must have been a treat. Kidd has an endless supply of modern but old-fashioned ideas that work. Once in a lifetime timelessness.
L.H.M.

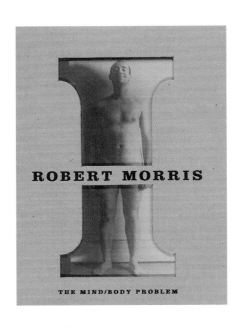

ROBERT MORRIS

THE MIND/BODY PROBLEM

Designers
J. Abbott Miller, David B. Williams

Editor
Rosalind Krauss

Photographers
Various

Design Firm
Design Writing Research

Client
Solomon R. Guggenheim Museum

Printer
Hull Printing

Paper
Monadnock Dulcet, raw binder's board

ENTRANT'S COMMENTS

This book on artist Robert Morris included scholarly essays as well as a large illustrated catalog. Morris has participated in several phases of contemporary art since the 1960s, including performance, conceptual art, minimalist sculpture, earthworks and painting. One thread throughout the artist's work is his preoccupation with the materiality of writing and language, underscored by his frequent use of a massive slab serif font. The design of the book unites the disparate styles of Morris's ouevre by recourse to the small-scale monumentality of the typeface Clarendon set against the more delicate and encyclopedic Garamond text face. The cover of the book recreates one of Morris's best known works, the I-Box. The capital I forms a die-cut door which opens to reveal a naked self-portrait. The use of raw binder's board for the cover refers to Morris's exploration of impoverished raw materials such as felt and plywood.

JURORS' COMMENTS

There sure are a lot of ideas here. Exposed cloth, rough cardboard, the die cut, the foil stamping: it's a bit exhausting. But you can't not open this cover. You've just got to see whether there's a pay-off. The artwork is handled masterfully: it's allowed to be as big as it needs to be. There's a lot of breathing space so you don't feel overwhelmed. The essays are designed really smartly — not too dense, even though there's an awful lot of information. S.D.

This is a beautiful, well organized book. The designer deeply understands the art of the opening sequence. This book is like walking into a grand lobby — totally awesome. L.H.M.

5 8

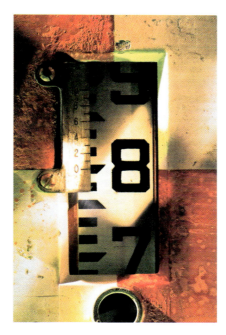

DESIGNERS
Jennifer Jerde, Mark Winn

WRITER
Paula Mangin

PHOTOGRAPHER
Tony Stromberg

DESIGN FIRM
Elixir Design Company

CLIENT
San Francisco Show

PRINTER
Watermark/Express Quality Printing

SEPARATOR
Pacific Digital Imaging

PAPER
Simpson Coronado SST

ENTRANT'S COMMENTS

Each year, the San Francisco Ad Club and the San Francisco Creative Alliance host a competition for the best advertising and design in the Bay Area. Judges are flown in from other parts of the country to evaluate the city's creative work, the results of which are displayed in a gala event and a commemorative annual. By focusing on San Francisco (from the point of view of the country as a whole) we found a very flexible vehicle for presenting the event. The city's "erratic" topography provided an easily understood, mildly humorous metaphor for a survey to assess "the Bay Area's creative landscape." (Steep competition.) By blending elements drawn from land surveying (tools, topographic maps, etc.) with the notion of plotting ones' observations (from afar), we felt the event was metaphorically captured.

JURORS' COMMENTS

I like how these march on and keep delivering the same idea with excruciating accuracy. It's a nice theme, it's handsome, it's graphic. It seems to have a sense of humor and doesn't take itself too seriously. But the fun is in the precision. **S.D.**

The visual references are all types of measuring devices, a light-hearted commentary on the meaning of an awards show. **L.H.M.**

Bronzo

DESIGNER
Rick Valicenti

WRITERS
Rick Valicenti, Todd Lief

ILLUSTRATORS
Rick Valicenti, Mark Rattin, Tony Klassen

DESIGN FIRM
Thirst

CLIENT
Thirstype

TYPOGRAPHER
Thirst

PRINTER/SEPARATOR
TCR

PAPER
Gilbert

ENTRANT'S COMMENTS

Codify and sell the Bronzo collection.

JURORS' COMMENTS

This pamphlet contains the designer's inspired illustrations in addition to the Thirst typeface collection. Rick continues to contribute a wild energy to the dialogue of design styles. Rick is still riffing — more way out than ever. **L.H.M.**

What I like about Valicenti's type promotions is that he makes type look like a highly valuable asset. With so many major type foundries discounting fonts while scrambling to survive, Rick's approach of objectifying typefaces by means of these entertaining booklets is both refreshing and, in the long run, perhaps the only way for type foundries to survive. **R.V.D.L.**

Glycomed Inc.

1993 Annual Report

DESIGNER
Jean Orlebeke

ART DIRECTOR
Bill Cahan

WRITERS
Julie Wood, Carole Melis

PHOTOGRAPHER
Anthony Pardines

DESIGN FIRM
Cahan and Associates

CLIENT
Glycomed Inc.

PRINTER
Anderson Litho

PAPER
Karma

ENTRANT'S COMMENTS

Glycomed's two primary goals for this annual report were to emphasize the strength of their science team and to report on the progress and positive results of their products in pre-clinical tests. The book is organized around the company's three research areas. For each area we included a portrait of a scientist and their statement regarding the potential of a particular compound, product status charts, photography showing before and after treatment of lab results, and a diagram illlustrating how the product works. We sought to portray a company that balances strong scientific leadership with unique product applications.

JURORS' COMMENTS

This has all the good qualities of traditional annual reports, including clear thinking and the good sense to put the logo on the back. I am drawn to the beautiful and informative diagrams of cells. **L.H.M.**

I'm still a sucker for perfectly crafted graphic design. The dynamic typography, the modestly used photography, the restrained yet effective usage of color, the narrow format, the beautiful diagrams, the perfect printing... It almost made me want to read it, but instead I find myself just drooling over the well-crafted details. **R.V.D.L.**

**Indiana Arts Commission
Arts in Education**

Technical Assistance Guide

DESIGNERS
James Sholly, Laura Lacy-Sholly

WRITER
Skip Berry

COORDINATOR
Angie Dunfee

DESIGN FIRM
Antenna

CLIENT
Indiana Arts Commission

PRINTER
Print Communications, Inc.

PAPER
Beveridge Railroad Board, Hopper Kiana

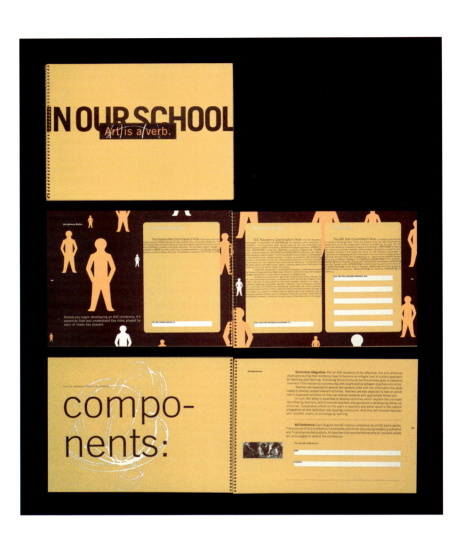

ENTRANT'S COMMENTS

This informational workbook is part of the Indiana Arts Commission's ongoing effort to integrate graphic design into conventionally dry governmental publications. This piece acts as a guide and instructional manual for the Arts in Education program which integrates art and artists into the kindergarten through twelfth grade curriculums. An example of this is teaching students about science through the use of modern dance. The design of this piece takes its visual cues from grade school culture and imagined bureaucratic ephemera.

JURORS' COMMENTS

This is a workbook for community involvement in the schools. Using energetic type and color, the printed piece may actually influence participation and dialog among diverse groups. L.H.M.

I can't deny picking this one because of the title. This is a crucial issue, and the design does a great job getting its message across without being artsy fartsy. Nonetheless, the designers have left their mark with creative use of color, loose and reader-friendly typography, and nicely paced page layouts. R.V.D.L.

DESIGNER
Neal Ashby

WRITER
Fred Guthrie

ILLUSTRATOR
Dave Plunkert

PHOTOGRAPHER
Steve Biver

DESIGN FIRM/CLIENT
**Recording Industry
Association of America**

PRINTER
Steckel

PAPER
Starwhite Vicksburg

ENTRANT'S COMMENTS

While going through some of the RIAA's historical documents, I found a copy of our 1963 annual report. Apparently, it was made in-house. The cover was manila kraft paper with the title typed on a sticker. It had a quality of simplicity that made it seem honest and non-slick. I tried to keep the spirit of that annual report in mind when designing the 1993 version, which tried to tackle subjects as diverse as the future of digital musical delivery and CD piracy. The visual theme of the book is really about "old vs. new." Only two typefaces were used: New Baskerville (old) and Matrix (new). Dave Plunkert's illustrations use old images, rearranged to create something new. The wrapper with the woman with her hand to her ear represents the old way of listening to music, while underneath, the cyborg-like illustration represents the new media of digital music delivery.

JURORS' COMMENTS

Using nostalgic imagery and type, this strange and beautiful piece promotes the recording industry as one whose future is evolving directly from its past, but not without a hint of sentimentality for the "good old days." L.H.M.

This report shows a rather curious combination of images which are nearly antithetical in character. One type shows us a "Brazil" type of future through nostalgic looking collages, while the other offers slick, state-of-the-art full color photography. The typography follows suit using a combination of classical and contemporary typefaces in a layout that is familiar yet slightly askew. With one foot planted in the past and the other in the future, this is a pretty successful solution. R.V.D.L.

DESIGNER
Christopher Vice

WRITER
Marco Cenzatti

PHOTOGRAPHER
Peter Alexander

DESIGN FIRM
Christopher Vice

CLIENT
Los Angeles Forum for Architechture
and Urban Design

TYPOGRAPHER
Christopher Vice

PRINTER
George Little Press

PAPER
Gilbert Esse, Vintage Velvet

ENTRANT'S COMMENTS

Marco Cenzatti's monograph establishes a context for
strategies of restructuring that reveal the prominence
of over-lapping marginal narratives and expose the
inadequacy of Modernism's dominant culture models.
The author intended his ideas to link four seminal
essays. Though these texts could not be reprinted, their
conceptual necessity demanded some significant
device. They exist as opaque volumes sprawling like
the Southern California landscape. The design explores
notions of centrality, marginality, difference and
plurality through subtle shifts and tensions. Typefaces
act as totems to L.A.'s economic booms which inscribed
the city's character. The book is illustrated with
impressions of the 1992 L.A. uprisings.

JURORS' COMMENTS

Elliptical lines swinging through columns of type, academic editorial elements and surprising imagery combine to
make this piece a rich reading treat. L.H.M.

If people are worried about the future of print, they should get a copy of this exquisite catalog. The relationship
between the sprawling typography, end of the world images and texts is so solidly intertwined, it nearly smells like Los Angeles.
This is very inspiring work, showing us a myriad of typographic possibilities to explore. R.V.D.L.

Muse: A Visual Recording

DESIGNERS
Matt Fey, Steve Gariepy, Ed Wantuch

WRITERS
John Gehner, Tiffany Root,
Michelle Judge, Matt Fey,
Steve Gariepy, Ed Wantuch

ILLUSTRATORS
Matt Fey, Steve Gariepy, Ed Wantuch

DESIGN FIRM/CLIENT
Muse

PRINTER
Microprint

PAPER
Fox River Confetti, Gilbert Gilclear

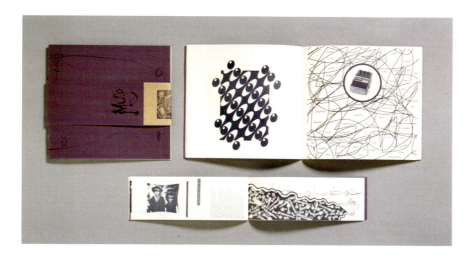

ENTRANT'S COMMENTS

Muse was inspired by the parallels that exist between different genres of art, specifically between graphic art and music. Structurally modeled after an audio recording, the piece is a compilation of individual "singles" — solo as well as collaborative works "recorded" onto a format consisting of a large book that is wrapped with a smaller sealed book. The two books, and the pieces within, are designed to interact with and play off one another. This, our second self-published release, is another step toward focusing our concept of a visual recording.

JURORS' COMMENTS

In the spirit of great experimentation, the piece looks like the magazine equivalent of the sounds of a good garage band. Who isn't rocked by that? **L.H.M.**

Designers should allow themselves time to be involved with these self-exploratory pieces to keep those creative muscles in shape at all times. There has to be an outlet when the Muse comes calling. This is a very entertaining piece. Within music, graphic design is usually subservient, only there to sell or announce the music. This project sort of turns the tables. I enjoy reading and looking at this, wondering what music would best serve the graphics. **R.V.D.L.**

DESIGNERS
Somi Kim, Susan Parr, Whitney Lowe, Lorraine Wild, Caryn Aono, Andrea Fella

EDITOR
Miyoshi Barosh

DESIGN FIRM
ReVerb, Los Angeles

CLIENT
Miyoshi Barosh; A.R.T.* Press

TYPOGRAPHERS
Somi Kim, Susan Parr, Whitney Lowe, Lorraine Wild, Caryn Aono, Andrea Fella, Ed Fella

PRINTER
Delta Graphics

PAPER
Topkote Gloss, Lustro Saxony

ENTRANT'S COMMENTS

Now Time is an eclectic magazine that combines art, design, architecture, film, music and new writing with interviews and new projects. This issue, number 3, is the artificial intelligence issue. Unlike most periodicals, **Now Time** has avoided a standardized format and changes not only from issue to issue, but also from piece to piece. We imposed stricter parameters of grids and typefaces to this issue (as compared to previous issues) to achieve the appearance of a scientific journal, but the design of each piece was based on a close reading of the material and discussions with the editor.

JURORS' COMMENTS

This magazine supports experimental graphic design, writing and adventurous subject matter. Many different designers develop spreads separately; the articles are then assembled into a bumper-to-bumper, collision-bound highway to new ideas and visual form. **L.H.M.**

It's too bad Now Time isn't distributed more widely. I wish we could see this combination of intelligence, humor and typographic excellence influence other magazines. Of course, the work involved in treating each separate article with such care and thoughtfulness might simply be too great for magazines published on a weekly or monthly basis. I am in awe, also, to see this many designers working together to create something completely cohesive. **R.V.D.L.**

DESIGNER
Andrew Blauvelt

WRITER
Christopher Scoates

DESIGN FIRM
Andrew Blauvelt

CLIENT
Atlanta College of Art Gallery

PRINTER
Theo Davis Sons, Inc.

PAPER
Springhill Tag

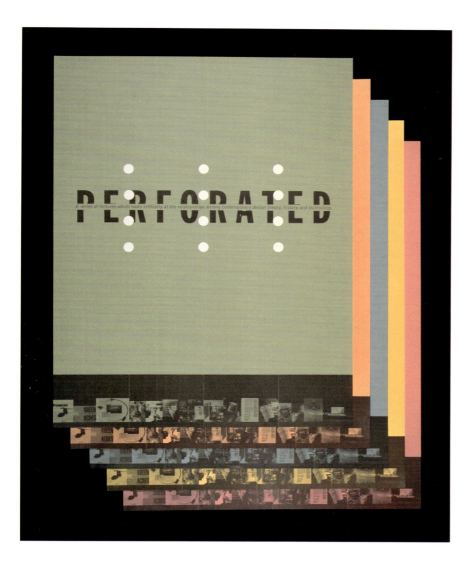

ENTRANT'S COMMENTS

"Perforated" is the metaphoric title for five lectures about graphic design and contemporary culture. The poster conveys two definitions of perforation: to bore holes for filtering and to puncture for detachment. Graphically, the die-cut holes of the poster and a series of removable cards along the bottom embody these ideas. The poster is printed on five different colored industrial papers and borrows its structure from those bulletin board notices with little tear-off telephone numbers. Specific lecture information appears on the back of each card.

JURORS' COMMENTS

This poster reflects some of the values of contemporary design: simple use of materials and language. The perforations suggest that the lecturers are punching through the status quo design culture. **L.H.M.**

I like the authoritative, literal representation of the word "perforated." It immediately demands your attention. The perforations suggest a probing into the subject matter presented by the lecturers, but also relate directly to the fact that although the lectures are part of a series they can easily be seen separately. **R.V.D.L.**

DESIGNERS
Allen Hori, Charlie Becker

WRITER
Augustine Hope

COORDINATION
The Kuester Group

PHOTOGRAPHERS
Allen Hori, Gaye Chan

DESIGN FIRM
Bates Hori

CLIENT
Potlatch Corporation

TYPOGRAPHERS
Allen Hori, Charlie Becker, Rob Eberhardt

PRINTER/SEPARATOR
Watt Peterson, Inc.

PAPER
Vintage Remarque

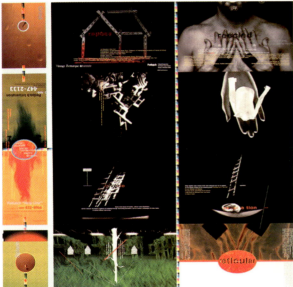

ENTRANT'S COMMENTS

Music is the most mysterious of the arts. This is an ode to music. In Australian creation myths, the world was sung into existence by the first man. Today, there remain some aborigines who can cross the continent on foot without a map. They navigate with ancestral songs that describe every topographical detail along the route — the songline — that they will take. Are these mnemonic maps, or is the singer creating the world anew each time? The creative act is a moment of pure energy, experienced as a sudden consonance of images which one rushes to consign to paper. Memory and dreams, chance and fate, doubt and certainty, events we have seen, heard or felt, all play a part in the process. Rooted in mathematics, music powerfully combines reason and intuition, weaving sound and silence, harmony, dissonance, rhythm and melody into a roadmap of the soul. Like the composer, the designer is a scavenger-artist.

JURORS' COMMENTS

I am moved by the poetic approach of this piece. The high level of abstraction is really something to be felt and seen. The complexity of the form itself, mastery of materials, printing and construction, and the self-generated imagery and text is simply a virtuoso presentation. **L.H.M.**

If there is any graphic designer today who has successfully blurred the lines between graphic design, writing and fine art, it is Allen Hori. His work continues to amaze me. Anything I might say would only diminish his creations. **R.V.D.L.**

DESIGNERS
Charles S. Anderson, Paul Hovalt

WRITER
Lisa Pemrick

PHOTOGRAPHER
Darrell Eager

DESIGN FIRM
**Charles S. Anderson
Design Company**

CLIENT
American Center for Design

PRINTER
RPP Enterprises

FILM
IPP LithoColor

PAPER
French Dur-o-tone

ENTRANT'S COMMENTS

When we were asked to design the ACD Student Conference Poster we felt it was our civic duty to inform students of the 1,200 colleges this poster went out to that the design profession is bursting at the seams. We photographed plastic graduation cake toppers after dousing them in sterno and lighting them on fire. The poster is entitled "First Degree Burn." Graphic design's popularity, combined with computer technology, has allowed everyone to call themselves graphic designers. Design is in danger of becoming a commodity. Unfortunately, most corporate clients seem to think that when they buy computers they are buying design capabilities and that all they need is an operator. As my Dad used to say, "It's the tail wagging the dog."

JURORS' COMMENTS

This very strong poster indicates a new direction for this designer, and projects great energy because of it. More photography, Chuck! **L.H.M.**

The notion put forward in this poster is rather sobering and poignant. Anderson couldn't have picked a more appropriate design job to replace his usual nostalgic clip art images with such telling photography. I'd like to see him do this a lot more. He's pretty good at it. **R.V.D.L.**

DESIGNER
Susan Silton

WRITERS
Catherine Lord, Maurice Berger, Charles Gaines

DESIGN FIRM
SoS, Los Angeles

CLIENT
UC Irvine Fine Arts Gallery

TYPOGRAPHER
Susan Silton

PRINTER
Delta Graphics

PAPER
Mohawk Superfine, Centura Dull,
French Dur-o-tone

ENTRANT'S COMMENTS

To document an exhibition and subsequent roundtable discussion with a modest printing budget, this catalog intends to reflect some of the critical discourse generated by mainstream press regarding the African-American artist. The result is a stark cover on which the title primarily has been blind debossed — the weight of language evident — except for the word "refusal," which appears in black. The interior of the book provides a structure in which to examine these issues. A white coated section stands apart from the body. Within this section, black and white photographs of the artists' work appear directly opposite quotations from critical sources, thus echoing the framework of the exhibition. Some of the quotations are pulled out in red for further emphasis.

JURORS' COMMENTS

I'm interested in the use of typographic oddities within a conventional format. I am seduced by the beautiful typography and care given the book, but I question the lack of cultural signifiers used to let the reader know the book is about black art. **L.H.M.**

You don't need big bucks to create something very elegant and attractive.

The cover, created with a minimum of means, immediately drew me in with its visual play of debossed and highlighted words which reinforce the title effectively. It takes a certain amount of self-confidence and self-control to present a critical issue in such a quiet and restrained way. **R.V.D.L.**

Burton Snowboards

1994 Dealer Catalog

DESIGNERS
David Covell, Dan Sharp, Keith Brown

CREATIVE DIRECTOR
Michael Jager

ART DIRECTOR
David Covell

DESIGN FIRM
Jager Di Paola
Kemp Design

CLIENT
Burton Snowboards

PRINTER
Danbury Printing

PAPER
Vintage Velvet

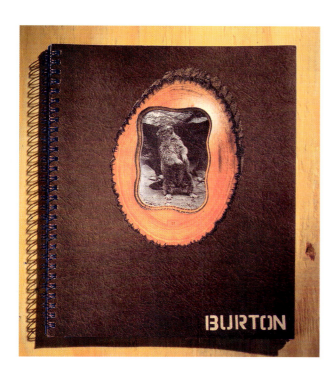

ENTRANT'S COMMENTS

This year, the market was flooded with upstart companies, all claiming to be the hippest. They all came with the latest computer tricks and type. To squelch these youngsters, we played up Burton's unique position in Vermont as well as their long history of innovation. We used a variety of hand-rendered type and visual references from our road trips to Vermont flea markets, tourist traps and deer camps to create this homegrown catalog. We tried to create a funky, spontaneous trip to the mountains with stops at authentic, well-crafted product along the way.

JURORS' COMMENTS

These guys got a lot of attention last year and I'm not sure that this is terribly different. It's still great fun, however. We're talking about it like it's some kind of design icon. But it's just so wonderfully stupid. Ralph Lauren should be really jealous of this because they take his idea of grave-robbing the vernacular and deliver it with much more energy and just whomp it with a snowboard. Too much fun. **S.D.**

This work has been quite influential over the past year. I noticed more than a few catalogs for large companies among the submissions to this show that were obviously inspired by this. Usually, the imitators end up doing a better job since they don't have to invest any effort to arrive at the results generated by the originators. They can simply concentrate on refining and improving. This time around, however, the copycats seem to be unable to keep that perfect balance between complete insanity and typographic mastery as do Jager Di Paola Kemp. And with Burton, there's just no letting up. The work still exudes excitement as if it was the first catalog they ever did. To continue to do this, time and again, without getting tiresome, is worth an award in and of itself. **R.V.D.L.**

COR Therapeutics

1993 Annual Report

DESIGNER
Jean Orlebeke

ART DIRECTOR
Bill Cahan

WRITER
Joyce Knapp

ILLUSTRATOR
Keith Kasnott

PHOTOGRAPHER
Robert Schlatter

DESIGN FIRM
Cahan & Associates

CLIENT
COR Therapeutics, Inc.

PRINTER
Graphic Arts Center

PAPER
Kashmir

ENTRANT'S COMMENTS

Each year we have included an educational section in the COR Annual Report which discusses issues related to cardiovascular disease. To reinforce COR's "we're in the clinic" message, we followed a patient through her cardiovascular experience. We incorporated patient records, a patient-doctor dialog, documentary-style photography and illustrated excerpts from the doctor's clinical notes. While not completely satisfied with the aesthetic outcome of this year's annual, we are committed to what this project represents: an opportunity to educate and deliver important information about heart disease.

JURORS' COMMENTS

They've tackled a difficult subject matter in a respectful way. It starts off with a lot of seductive and clinical typography. But then, before you know it, you're drawn into this narrative. It's beautifully detailed and cross-referenced between the micro-photography, the action shots and the diagrams and stuff. It's a great package of information. It's got a gorgeous story-telling voice that took me by surprise. **S.D.**

The patient profile and day-by-day case study presented as a foldout tucked away in a file folder complete with tabs gives this **a dimension seldom seen in annual reports.** It's almost a bit overdone, but I would imagine that COR stockholders are well served by this very insightful and educational publication. **R.V.D.L.**

DESIGNER
Matt Eller

WRITER
Nancy Roth

EDITOR
Phil Freshman

DESIGN FIRM/CLIENT
Walker Art Center

TYPOGRAPHER
Matt Eller

PRINTER
Insty Prints

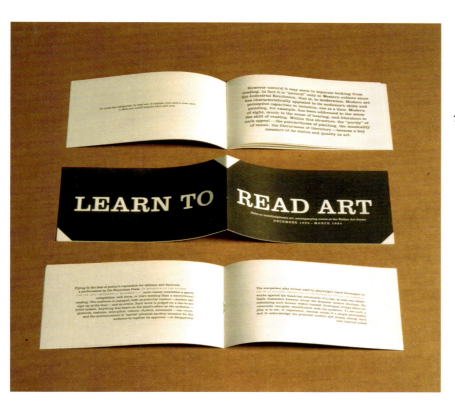

ENTRANT'S COMMENTS

The Walker Art Center's recent exhibition of Lawrence Weiner posters was an opportunity to create a small brochure framed by the deceptively simple phrase "Learn To Read Art." By collaborating with a writer, I was able to explore the "look" of language and the way that sequence and format influence the reading of a given text. The multi-voiced discussion is illuminated by subtle typographic shifts.

JURORS' COMMENTS

There's something a bit juvenile or primary school about it, which is its charm, given the subject matter. It's a reference to the books we used to have in school, which were, of course, bigger. We're given a piece of it to recall. The type is nicely detailed. A little bit funky, a little bit playful, but not offputting. **S.D.**

Simple and endearing. Looks like one of those "form follows budget" projects. **R.V.D.L.**

Poster

DESIGNER
P. Scott Makela

3D MODELING
Alex Tylevich

PHOTOGRAPHER
Rik Sferra

DESIGN FIRM
Words+Pictures

CLIENT
American Center for Design

FILM
Laser Graphics

PRINTER
Unique Printers and Lithographers

PAPER
Hammermill Opaque

ENTRANT'S COMMENTS

Trying to find an entry point into "new media" is a
challenge to many graphic and industrial designers.
This poster opted to portray a future where technology
and human flesh suggest powerful new tools and
territories for investigation. Cable TV scramble and a
muscular neck seek negotiation with each other.
The red, green and blue (RGB) ball has been a symbol
for the electronic surface since the advent of color TV.
The "tongue" of flame represents the ignition of passion.

JURORS' COMMENTS

I bought into this thing partly to baffle my detractors. It's important to acknowledge how "of the moment"
this design is. Scott Makela has captured the energy that is taking place in multimedia. It parallels
what's going on in cyberspace. It's a scintillating circus. It's joyous and free and fun, and it completely mystifies
me. It's amazing (and terrifying) how this stuff all colludes and congeals on the surface. My God! S.D.

Type and image in motion frozen in time. There's a great deal of excitement going on in multimedia and this poster
relates that perfectly. Some of the type treatments might perhaps require a few extra seconds to read, but the
resulting vibrancy of the overall design draws me in immediately. Makela's experiments with electronic design
continue to signify that uneasy period that design now occupies, caught between the static nature of print and the
new possibilities offered by on-screen graphics. R.V.D.L.

The Marmon Group

1994 Annual Brochure

DESIGNERS
James Koval, Jo-Ann Boutin

WRITER
John Harris

ILLUSTRATORS
Bill Graham, Ilene Robinette

PHOTOGRAPHER
Howard Bjornson

DESIGN FIRM
VSA Partners, Inc.

CLIENT
The Marmon Group

PRINTER/SEPARATOR
The Hennegan Company

PAPER
French Dur-o-tone, Lustro Dull

ENTRANT'S COMMENTS

The Marmon Group is an international association of more than 60 autonomous companies that engage in a wide variety of manufacturing, industrial and service businesses. Many products produced by member companies are industry staples. The approach of this annual brochure is direct, educational and honest, while the design reflects the origins and diversity of The Marmon Group.

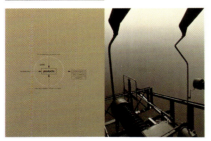

JURORS' COMMENTS

I like this annual report because it is so gleefully dull. It celebrates the ordinary in a winking and knowing way. The charts are wonderfully chart-like. They're not self-conscious in their self-consciousness. There's contradiction in the planes of the typography and a great color sense. There are bar charts doing what they do best unapologetically, and then an array of wacky stuff like the lawyer photograph and the pictures of the eggs and this fabulous map. It's delightful. It never goes overboard, it never gets sappy. It holds its line of integrity, somehow. **S.D.**

Although the cover is not its strength, the inside appeals to me a great deal. The crispness of the redrawn technical illustrations nicely tempers what could have been an extremely nostalgic look. Altogether it has an instruction book/science magazine quality to it that makes it accessible and trustworthy. **R.V.D.L.**

DESIGNERS
Sheridan Lowrey, Nicholas Lowie

DESIGN FIRM
Lowie/Lowrey Design

CLIENT
Southern California Institute of Architecture

PRINTER
Typecraft

PAPER
Matrix

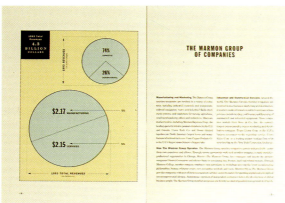

ENTRANT'S COMMENTS

Notwithstanding our having a personal relationship as editors to the essays submitted, affectations for each of the thirteen essays were determined by an over-privileged knowledge of architectural erudition. Superficial forms followed stylized functions. Dispensing contextualism but reinforcing language, we were concerned with the style of content (functions of semantic form which change systematically in value as fortuitous values change), rather than the investigation of the style-book of contemporaneity. Having replaced one stylistic concern for another complicates our respective audience's reception of the design: the palpable reader, oblivious of complacency to the requisite contemporary decoration, will be unaware of our attempt to fraternize in the style of rhetoric.

JURORS' COMMENTS

I hate loving this thing, but it's very seductive. They're going to give me a lot of grief at the office when they see my name next to this. (Can you imagine having dinner with these people?) It's a gorgeous version of this dense hypertextural stuff and really quite beautiful. **S.D.**

Like Chris Vice's "Los Angeles and the L.A. School" catalog, Offramp travels down a typographic path that I believe was first opened up by Lorraine Wild and Laurie Haycock Makela. It uses highly unusual typeface combinations and rather complex typographic structures as well as an extremely intense emphasis on detail. You better enjoy reading and you better have 20/20 eyesight because this magazine won't go easy on you. At least the cover warns you what to expect inside. **R.V.D.L.**

Petroleum

Book

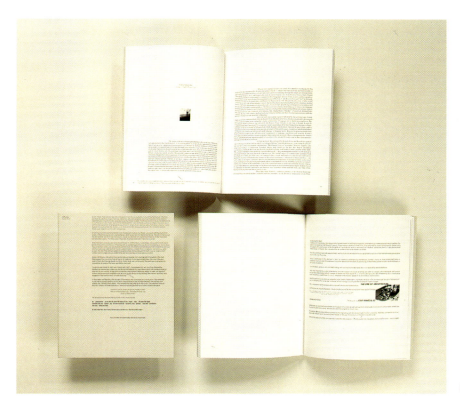

DESIGNER
Tom Wood

WRITER
Mary Anne Costello

PHOTOGRAPHER
Jeff Corwin

DESIGN FIRM
Wood Design

CLIENT
Louis Dreyfus Energy

TYPOGRAPHER
Tom Wood

PRINTER/SEPARATOR
The Hennegan Company

PAPER
Potlatch Karma, Simpson Starwhite Vicksburg

ENTRANT'S COMMENTS

This book was conceived to establish Louis Dreyfus Energy as a supplier, marketer and distributor of petroleum and natural gas and reflects an efficient, straightforward and progressive image built on 150 years of experience in most of the world's commodities markets. The company is understated by nature so there needed to be a clear and honest approach to the design and content. We accomplished a balance of innovation and tradition through the unconventional use of typography, materials, inks and surfaces which gave the book both warmth and an industrial edge. Strong black and white documentary photography symbolizes the essence of the subject. Sophisticated colors reflect both natural and industrial elements and an underlying grid of stability was punctuated by visual highlights consisting of a typographic collage, charts and map.

JURORS' COMMENTS

We have been looking at a lot of design that is hybrid, cross-bred and even inbred. I love the simplicity of this book, an artful arrangement of gorgeous, narrative photographs with type that is pristine and **unencumbered by self-consciousness.** This book is an oasis of calm, interspersing quietly colored stock with bright white pages which add up to the powerful telling of a story. Masterful in its reserve. **S.D.**

No flashy Photoshop images, no gimmicky typography, no hip fonts. This project just stands rock solid among a lot of self-indulgent and pretentious graphic design. **R.V.D.L.**

The Romancing of Rome

DESIGNER
Robert Fisher

CLIENT
Krannert Art Museum

TYPOGRAPHER
Robert Fisher

PRINTER
United Graphics

SEPARATOR
ScanTech

PAPER
Hopper Proterra

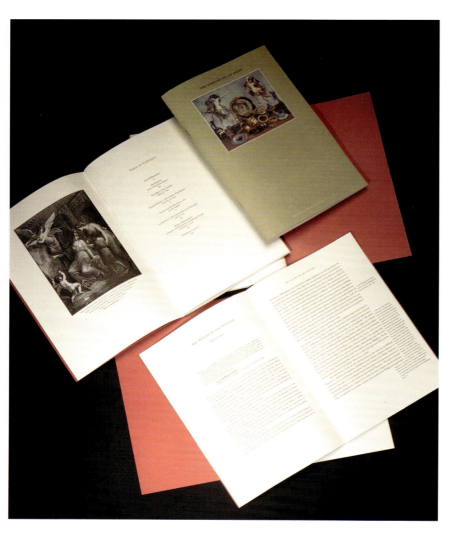

ENTRANT'S COMMENTS

The exhibition for which this catalog was produced drew upon the recurring themes of classicism found in 18th, 19th and 20th century architecture, landscape architecture and the fine and decorative arts. In consideration of these historical references, the design of the catalog is based on an interpretation of classicism in typography and book arts. My intention was to create a context well suited for the understanding of historicism discussed in the catalog's essays while exemplifying the timeless beauty of classicism.

JURORS' COMMENTS

I'm not crazy about the cover. It seems to miss a chance to signal some of the richness inside. But I love the footprint of the textbox on the page. The thing that knocked me out was the wraparound margin area on page two. There are a couple of other spreads in here that are particularly beautiful. It's quite textural in a simple, classical and neat way. And it's not overproduced. It's refreshing. Very successful and very slow. **S.D.**

This starts off so innocently and understated on the cover, but as soon as you open it up and face the off-center title page you know you're in for something special. From there on, typographically, the book is completely entertaining, building and adding onto its structure, getting quite elaborate without ever getting dense. **R.V.D.L.**

The **100**[+2] show

Selections by:
Stephen Doyle

DESIGNERS
Pat and Greg Samata

WRITER
Liz Horan

PHOTOGRAPHER
Marc Norberg

DESIGN FIRM
Samata Associates

CLIENT
American Heart Association
of Metropolitan Chicago

TYPOGRAPHER
Dan Kraemer

PRINTER/SEPARATOR
Columbia Graphics

PAPER
French Dur-o-tone

ENTRANT'S COMMENTS

The American Heart Association of Metropolitan Chicago
is in the business of saving lives. In its 1993 annual
report we profiled three people most likely to fall into
high risk categories for cardiovascular disease and
heart attacks. We combined symbolic photography and
bold type treatment with photos of researchers
instrumental in fighting stroke and heart disease.

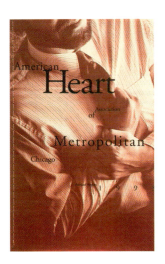

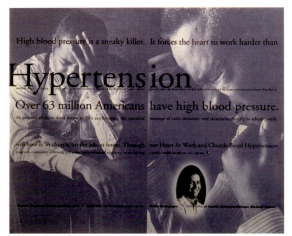

JUROR'S COMMENTS

This is one of the first things that I noticed. I was really moved. The typography has actually charged the statistics.
It looks benign, but upon reading it you get a shock. Nice delivery. **S.D.**

DESIGNER
David Carson

EDITOR
Andrea Danese

PHOTOGRAPHER
Albert Watson

TYPOGRAPHER
David Carson

DESIGN FIRM
David Carson Design

PUBLISHER
Bulfinch

PRINTER
Heritage Press

SEPARATOR
Richard Benson

PAPER
Lustro Dull

JUROR'S COMMENTS

How did David Carson convince Albert Watson to accept a type cover for a book of photographs? It's gorgeous! It's immediate. It's compelling. Open the cover and already he's up to his typo-tricks: the flap copy continues onto the endpapers, cleaving a column of body copy in two. This book has been Carson-ized™ just enough to infuse it with personality, but not so much as to interfere. The pictures are paired expertly. And don't miss Hitchcock holding that fowl carcass! **S.D.**

First Nonprofit Companies

Brochure

DESIGNERS
Kerry Grady, Heather Miller

WRITER
Lynne Hepler

PHOTOGRAPHER
Jean Moss

DESIGN FIRM
Grady, Campbell
Incorporated

CLIENT
First Nonprofit Companies

TYPOGRAPHER
Paul Baker

PRINTER/SEPARATOR
First Impression

PAPER
Neenah Classic Crest

ENTRANT'S COMMENTS

First Nonprofit Companies insures nonprofit associations and small businesses in the midwest. This book was designed to act as an introduction to the company and the products it offers. Our approach was to be sensible, tasteful and affordable. This piece helps to position First Nonprofit Companies as a leader in their business and as a people-oriented company, exemplified through photography that features real customers who benefit from its services.

JUROR'S COMMENTS

This understated brochure is a real magnet for me. The scale accounts for its presence, and the lean typography gives it confidence. Jean Moss is the perfect photographer for these easy-going family album kind of portraits. It comes together in a way that looks both effortless and important. **S.D.**

Granges Inc.

1993 Annual Report

DESIGNER
Dave Mason

WRITER
Granges Inc.

ILLUSTRATOR
Pamela Lee

DESIGN FIRM
Dave Mason &
Associates Inc.

CLIENT
Granges Inc.

TYPOGRAPHER
Dave Mason & Associates Inc.

PRINTER
H. MacDonald Printing

PAPER
Simpson

ENTRANT'S COMMENTS

Granges Inc. explores, acquires, develops and operates
mineral properties in North America. Along with maps,
schematics and charts, the prime visual components
in the report are "word pictures" that were developed
to graphically introduce various sections of the book.
Each word picture is based on actual data sheets and
technical documents used in a particular area
of the company's business. The result is a kind of
understated visual puzzle that is engaging
both for laymen and those with more specific
knowledge of the mining industry.

JUROR'S COMMENTS

This thing really handsomely and intriguingly gets down to the silver, gold, zinc and copper or whatever they dig up.
I love the charting and the mapping of the financials. The maps are little gems, precise and
inviting to look at. S.D.

DESIGNERS
Dana Arnett, Ken Fox, Carlos Segura

WRITERS
Thomas Bolfert, Buzz Buzzelli, M. Bruce Chubbuck,
Martin Jack Rosenblum

DESIGN FIRM
VSA Partners, Inc.

CLIENT
Harley-Davidson, Inc.

PRINTER
HM Graphics, Inc.

SEPARATOR
Lithographics, Inc.

PAPER
Champion Kromekote and Carnival

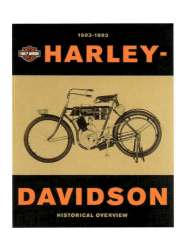

ENTRANT'S COMMENTS

The Harley-Davidson 90th anniversary book gives
an historical overview of the motorcycles built by
Harley-Davidson from 1903 to 1993. This 160-page book
includes over 150 black and white archival photographs
representing the background and heritage of this
unique American institution.

JUROR'S COMMENTS

I'm really attracted to Dana's **cavalcade of typography.** This is one time and place where a banged up typeface really works, especially when you slam it on an introduction page against the words Harley-Davidson scrawled on the door of an outhouse. It presents itself as a well-researched history book. It would be great to spend time with it. It's a really dynamic layout that gives you the feeling of the evolution of Harley-Davidson. It's under-produced just enough and the cover feels swell. **S.D.**

LinoGraphics

Price Guide

DESIGNER
William Kochi

PHOTOGRAPHER
William Kochi

DESIGN FIRM
KODE Associates, Inc.

CLIENT
LinoGraphics

PRINTER
Otis Graphics

SEPARATOR
LinoGraphics

PAPER
Neenah Buckskin, Gilbert Oxford

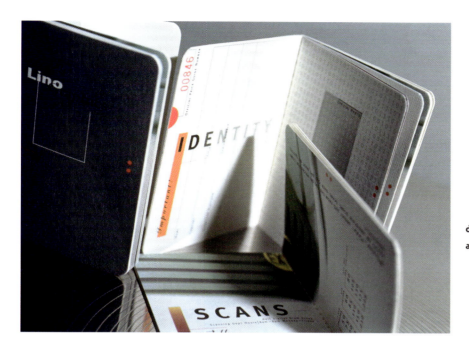

ENTRANT'S COMMENTS

Perhaps the only thing worse than having to read a price list is having to design one. We came up with the idea to combine a promotional device and a functional business necessity into one convenient reference guide. While all images were taken with a digital camera, most of the client's services were taken advantage of to produce the price guide electronically. In the end, the smythe-sewn binding added more character to the final product.

JUROR'S COMMENTS

How much material is really needed to get across a given amount of information? This stands out because of its odd little size and nutty graphics. It takes detailed information and gives it some whiz-bang. S.D.

DESIGNER
Brain Wu, Toshiya Masuda

EDITOR
Christopher Cardozo

PHOTOGRAPHER
Edward S. Curtis

DESIGN FIRM
Callaway Editions, Inc.

PUBLISHER
Bulfinch

TYPOGRAPHER
Toshiya Masuda

PRINTER
Heritage Press

SEPARATOR
Richard Benson

PAPER
Mohawk Vellum

ENTRANT'S COMMENTS

Native Nations is a magnificent distillation of the best of photographer/ethnographer/adventurer Edward S. Curtis's landmark twenty-volume study of the Indian peoples at the turn of the century. As our intention overall was to be neutral both in design and in stance, we chose not to employ typography drawn from that period. Instead the typefaces used, Meridien and Trajan, are modern interpretations of classical Roman forms. Similarly, the image sequencing is based on themes and visual relationships, rather than on geography as in previous editions. Images were juxtaposed on facing pages only when this enhanced both in an aesthetic context. The paper, cover material and colors, however, were meant to simulate those of earlier editions of Curtis prints.

JUROR'S COMMENTS

One of the judges reviewed this book and then dismissed it, disdaining the kerning between a raised cap and the text on the flap. This book is not about kerning. It is about preservation: the documentation of disappearing nations of people, as well as the preservation (through replication) of the photographic documents. The images are exquisite, powerful portraits. The layouts are handsome, restrained and sensitive. And look at the reproduction! Callaway Editions, in their inimitable style, pushes electronic pre-press to new boundaries (quadratones printed crystal-raster on uncoated stock) in order to re-create the look of flat-plate gravure. But don't let this formal praise get in the way of understanding the significance of producing a book like this — as a trade book no less. The hell with letterspacing; this is important work.
S.D.

DESIGNERS
Andrew Blauvelt, Jeff Rooney

WRITER
Ken Friedlein

PHOTOGRAPHERS
Bob Donnan and various

DESIGN FIRM
Andrew Blauvelt

CLIENT
North Carolina State University
School of Design

PRINTER
Theo Davis Sons, Inc.

PAPER
Gilbert Esse

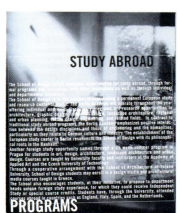

ENTRANT'S COMMENTS

This catalog serves to document student work done at
North Carolina State University's School of Design.
The recurring use of five squares represents the five
departments: architecture, design, graphic design,
industrial design and landscape architecture. Divider
pages were created by photographing different aspects
of the school. These images were collaged together
blindly in the camera by double-exposing rolls of
film. The empty chairs that appear on the covers are
found in the main critique room of the school and are
used symbolically as a gesture for entry and
participation in school life.

JUROR'S COMMENTS

I found this to be one of the strongest versions of its genre: intriguing and straight-forward. It's very architectural
in its programming. Believable, authoritative and exuberant. S.D.

DESIGNER
Bruce Mau with Nigel Smith

EDITOR
Harry F. Mallgrave

PHOTOGRAPHERS
John Kiffe, Jobe Benjamin

DESIGN FIRM
Bruce Mau Design

CLIENT
The Getty Center for the History
of Art and the Humanities

TYPOGRAPHER
Archetype

PRINTER/SEPARATOR
Bradbury Tamblyn & Boorne Ltd.

PAPER
Mohawk Navajo

ENTRANT'S COMMENTS

This, the third book in the Getty Center's Issues and
Debates series, continues and expands upon elements
and strategies developed in the first two. The formal
device used on the series book jackets is an extreme
figure/ground contrast. This device metaphorically
carries the book's exploration of the variant and
seemingly contradictory natures of the architect's
work. Was Wagner a traditionalist designer with
imperial ambitions or an avant garde modernist with a
penchant for iconography? This jacket design
dramatically contrasts a large photographic modern
detail and a small traditional drawing of the Vienna
Post Office. Hue, chroma and color are used throughout
the book to create internal resonance. Subtle
color variations are used to highlight key illustrations.
The metallic inks reflect the sensualist tendencies
of the architecture.

JUROR'S COMMENTS

This is beautiful. A book like this is an incredible undertaking and a delight to look at. There's nothing wrong with a really handsome, consistent set of books. It takes stamina to pull this off. I don't think you need to steer it in a different direction every year just because some designers are getting bored. I would hope that the audience is a little bit bigger and has a longer memory so that you can actually make a set of books that works as a set over one's lifetime. The great thing about books as opposed to magazines is that they last. Maybe they should be designed to last. **S.D.**

Takashimaya NY

Opening Mailer

DESIGNERS
Allison Muench, J.P. Williams

WRITER
Laura Silverman

PHOTOGRAPHER
Geof Kern

DESIGN FIRM
m/w: design

CLIENT
Takashimaya NY

PRINTER/SEPARATOR
Daniels Printing

PAPER
French Dur-o-tone, Monadnock Dulcet, Warren Lustro Dull, Bogus, Onionskin

ENTRANT'S COMMENTS

A catalog/brochure to create interest, awareness and above all curiosity. Conceived as an artist's travel scrapbook, this hardcover portfolio is filled with textures and viewpoints (newsprint, glossy, surrealism, onionskin, romantic pictorialism) that echo the mixture of cultures and creations throughout the store.

JUROR'S COMMENTS

This might actually be more fun than the store itself, and the store is a blast. It reminds me of going into a studio and examining all of the stuff on the wall. It's a delight to go from postcard to clipping. You wonder what the connection is. **There's an implied narrative between elements** and you're left to fill in the missing pieces yourself. Visual bonbons! It's extravagantly produced, but I think that pays off given what they're trying to project about the store. S.D.

The **IOO**$^{+2}$ show

Selections by:
Laurie Haycock Makela

DESIGNER
Rebeca Méndez

PHOTOGRAPHERS
John Kiffe, Jobe Benjamin

CLIENT
The Getty Center for the History
of Art and the Humanities

PRINTER/SEPARATOR
Monarch Litho Inc.

ENTRANT'S COMMENTS

The Getty Center for the History of Art and the
Humanities is dedicated to advanced research in the
history of art. Their scholars "reexamine the meaning
of art and artifacts within past and present cultures
and reassess their importance within the full scope of
the humanities and social sciences." To represent the
notion of reassessment, I chose a piece from the Getty's
collection by Fluxus artist George Brecht that states
"This sentence is weightless" in negative letterforms
cut from aluminum sheets. Language has no physical
weight, yet the meaning of words can have profound
weight. The photo of a man facing the horizon (Western
Avenue and Pico Boulevard, 1903) from J. Paul Getty's
personal scrapbook struck me as an historical moment
full of hope and anticipating the future. The overall
design emphasizes openness, which I believe to be
an essential requisite for scholarly inquiry.

JUROR'S COMMENTS

The fellowship program is like a secret club for scholars. To design a poster for the Center is a great opportunity to make very
esoteric allusions. By creating a floating sign, the designer has expressed an idea about how formless,
weightless language becomes visible. L.H.M.

1993 Annual Report

DESIGNERS
Pat and Greg Samata

WRITER
Allison McDonough

ILLUSTRATOR
Dugald Stermer

DESIGN FIRM
Samata Associates

CLIENT
DENTSPLY International, Inc.

TYPOGRAPHER
K.C. Yoon

PRINTER
Great Northern Printing

SEPARATOR
IPP LithoColor

PAPER
**Fox River Quality Cover Leather,
Neenah UV Ultra, Simpson Teton**

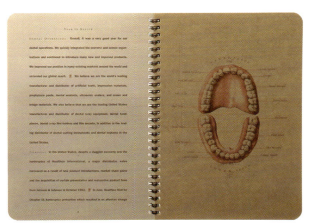

ENTRANT'S COMMENTS

DENTSPLY International leads the world in dental consumables and x-ray systems. The 1993 annual report is a simple fact book with an ongoing narrative interspersed with symbolic illustrations printed on a semitransparent parchment stock. We worked directly with the CEO to develop the fact book concept, a clear departure from previous more traditional annual reports.

JUROR'S COMMENTS

This elegant and tasteful annual report about dentistry uses a modest notebook cover to reduce the scale relative to the typical annual report. The clean parchment, photos, text and illustrations contribute toward an unusually warm presentation. **L.H.M.**

DESIGNERS
Neil Powell, Kobe

DESIGN FIRM
Duffy Design

CLIENT
Duffy Design

PRINTER
Reynolds Printing

PAPER
French Dur-o-tone, aluminum

ENTRANT'S COMMENTS

Creating a stationery system for a design firm can be very difficult. It is a statement about you and the way you approach your business. We build brands for the most part, so we thought it would be interesting if our stationery system had the graphic appearance of a branded product. Another challenging aspect was that it had to be cost-effective. The aluminium stamped business cards come with employee name stickers for personalization. And, of course, the card can be recycled.

JUROR'S COMMENTS

Stationery that attempts to be more than necessary usually fails, because the designer forgot that a letter may also end up on the page. This stationery, however, is so thorough in the way it takes into account the letter that I find it irresistible. **L.H.M.**

DESIGNER
Rafael Fajardo

WRITER
Rafael Fajardo

PHOTOGRAPHER
Rafael Fajardo

PRINTER
Tektronix Phaser IIIpsi

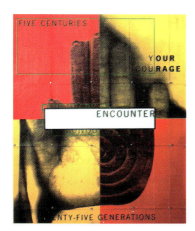
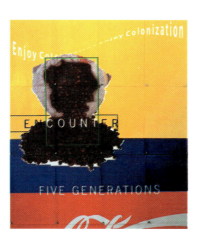

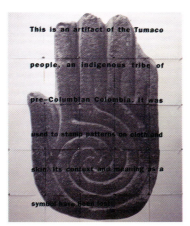

ENTRANT'S COMMENTS

This investigation was sparked by the five-hundredth anniversary of Columbus' voyage westward. I am juxtaposing representations of cultural, regional, corporate and personal identities. Through my work I establish a critical voice that communicates and explores the complexity of a contemporary sense of identity, where culture conflicts with money, power and bureaucracy which in turn conflict with human dignity. I question the divisiveness of the "multicultural" debate and would like to find a way in which two or more cultures can be represented equivocally, and not as one being a footnote to the other.

JUROR'S COMMENTS

I'm interested in this project because it studies cultural imagery and stereotyping. I wish that the final pieces reflected more of the designer's cultural heritage than that of contemporary European graphics. But it's honest and important research. **L.H.M.**

DESIGNER
Susan Silton

WRITERS
Kim Abeles, et al

ILLUSTRATOR
Kim Abeles

DESIGN FIRM
SoS, Los Angeles

CLIENT
Santa Monica Museum of Art
Fellows of Contemporary Art

TYPOGRAPHER
Susan Silton

PRINTER
Typecraft

PAPER
Vintage Velvet, Lexotone

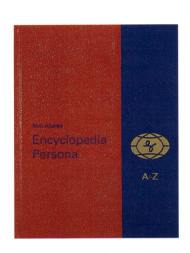

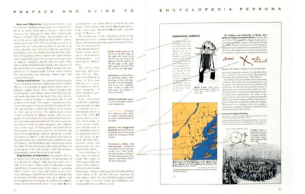

ENTRANT'S COMMENTS

The concept for Encyclopedia Persona resulted from the collaborative efforts of artist Kim Abeles, artist/graphic designer Susan Silton, and exhibition curator Karen Moss. Encyclopedia Persona is not an ordinary exhibition publication; it is a hybrid between an artist's book and a reference volume that serves as the catalog for Kim Abeles. The primary aims of this book are to fully illustrate Kim Abele's artistic production from 1979 to 1993; to provide an historical context for her work; and to chronicle her life as an artist, educator and activist in California during the past fifteen years. Modeled directly after an early 1960s edition of the World Book Encyclopedia, the objective of the publication is to present Abele's detailed investigations in a comprehensible format, using written text, photographs, line drawings, charts, maps and archival materials.

JUROR'S COMMENTS

This is a brilliant parody. Rarely is a reader treated to such a successful collaboration between artist, designer, curator and editor. **L.H.M.**

DESIGNER
Louise Sandhaus

CLIENT
Errant Bodies
California Institute of the Arts

PRINTER
Stacey Hauge

PAPER
Riegal Jersey, Simpson Coronado

ENTRANT'S COMMENTS

Literary and critical writing journals generally use a conventional design format. Conventional design is supposed to keep its mouth shut and do its job, which means it tries to be as invisible as possible so it doesn't interrupt the content. But design is never invisible or silent — you have to look through its voice in order to get to the content. Conventional design represents an ideology. Errant Bodies makes the convention burp here and there for readers who think that this type of design isn't doing anything to the content. The design of Errant Bodies is a noisy party for the signifiers of design.

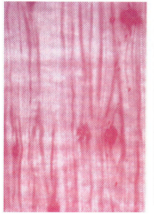

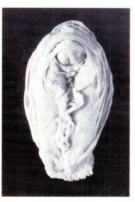

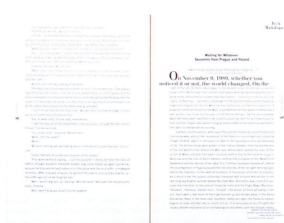

JUROR'S COMMENTS
I am interested in projects where designers and writers experiment together. The cover is odd and provocative. **L.H.M.**

FISEA '93

DESIGNER
Joseph D.R. O'Leary

DESIGN FIRM
Veto Design

CLIENT
Minneapolis College of Art and Design

TYPOGRAPHER
Joseph D.R. O'Leary

PRINTER/SEPARATOR
Bolger

PAPER
Centura Dull, Cougar

ENTRANT'S COMMENTS

The client wanted a "work of art" on a modest budget.
The statements and abstracts, collected from hundreds
of writers, artists, scientists and cyberpunks from
around the world were delivered to me (unedited)
ten days before final art was due at the printer.
At that point, I realized the layout needed to
accommodate to the constant changes, additions and
withdrawals. The images and edits poured in daily.
The clock was ticking and hallucinations took the
place of sleep, inadvertently adding an element of
surprise and chance to each spread. On the tenth
day it went to the printer. I went to sleep.

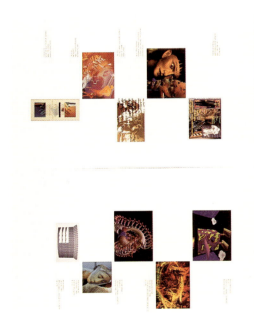

minneapolis
college of art
and design

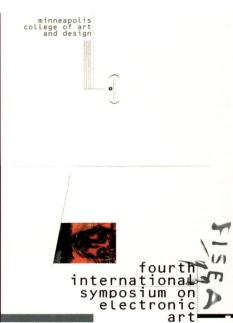

the art factor
exhibition

fourth
international
symposium on
electronic
art

FISEA

JUROR'S COMMENTS

There is lots of information in this big booklet for a conceptually big event. The type is strong and detailed. **L.H.M.**

DESIGNERS
Hal Wolverton, Alicia Johnson, Kat Saito

WRITER
Alicia Johnson

ILLUSTRATOR
Hal Wolverton

DESIGN FIRM
Johnson & Wolverton

CLIENT
AIGA/Portland

TYPOGRAPHER
Johnson & Wolverton

PRINTER
Bridgetown Printing

FILM
Agency Litho

PAPER
French Dur-o-tone

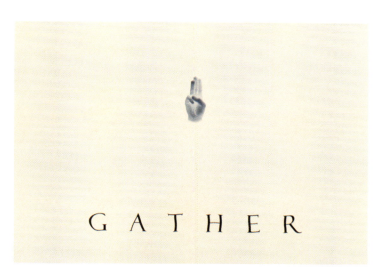

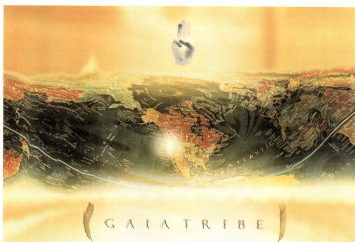

WANDERING THROUGH A SPIRITUAL AND CULTURAL WASTELAND
AT THE END OF THE 20TH CENTURY, AN UNPRECEDENTED NUMBER OF VISIONARIES CAME TOGETHER IN AN IDYLLIC RIVER VALLEY ON THE NORTHWEST RIM OF THE UNITED STATES, BOUND BY A COMMON QUEST FOR ANSWERS TO THE QUESTIONS OF THEIR TIME, THEIR CONNECTION TO THE PLACE, AND THEIR NEED TO BE HEARD, THIS TRIBE OF VISIONARIES BECAME KNOWN AS GAIATRIBE.

THIS COLLECTIVE CONCERN FOR PLACE (SEE ADOPT-A-TON), AND THE UNUSUAL VISION OF INDIVIDUAL TRIBE MEMBERS, LED TO INTERNATIONAL RECOGNITION OF GAIATRIBE. AS WAS THE FASHION OF THE TIME, AN 'ISM' WAS APPLIED TO THEIR PHILOSOPHY (THE MOVEMENT, GAISM, TRIBE MEMBERS, GAISTS). WITH INTERNATIONAL RECOGNITION CAME VISITING TRIBAL LEADERS, THROWING OPEN THE DOORS OF CREATIVE EXCHANGE. STARTED BY A LOOSE BAND OF COMMUNICATORS, THIS NEW MOVEMENT BROUGHT FOCUS AND JOY TO CREATORS THROUGHOUT THE LAND.

TODAY, THEIR RITUAL CONTINUES WITH AN ANNUAL HARVEST GATHERING TO CULMINATE A YEAR OF HARD WORK AND TOIL. A DESIGN INTERN IS SACRIFICED TO THE GOD OF INSPIRATION AS MEMBERS GATHER TO RENEW THEIR COMMITMENT, TO EXPAND THE TRIBE, AND TO HONOR THE PLACE THAT NURTURES THEIR VISION.

ENTRANT'S COMMENTS

For this invitation to an annual membership event, we created an allegorical example of what is possible in the Portland design community.

JUROR'S COMMENTS

This clever poster hails our return to tribal culture (oh, right!). It effectively evokes both technology and humanity.
L.H.M.

**Otis College of Art
and Design**

Catalog

DESIGNER
Lisa Nugent, Rick Vermeulen

PHOTOGRAPHY
Dennis Keeley

DESIGN FIRMS
ReVerb,
Hard Werken,
L.A. Desk

CLIENT
Otis College of Art and Design

TYPOGRAPHER
Lisa Nugent, Rick Vermeulen

PRINTER
Typecraft, Inc.

PAPER
Karma Matte, Monadnock

ENTRANT'S COMMENTS

The MFA catalog cover is designed to be a self-
mailer and is simple in its initial presentation.
Once the half-cover is opened, however, a colorful
interior is revealed and the reader is invited into
the text by visual surprises along the way. Holographic
and dark blue foils were used on the cover and
text as additional tidbits.

JUROR'S COMMENTS

This is a **truly freakish** use of materials and foil stamping. The colors are awkward; things don't go
together. That's graduate school. **L.H.M.**

DESIGNER
Heather Ferguson

WRITERS
Amy Jo Banton, Heather Ferguson, Brian Horner

ILLUSTRATORS
Amy Jo Banton, Edwin Uttermohlen

PROJECT COORDINATOR
Paula Differding

DESIGN FIRM
II Bellybuttons

CLIENT
Herron School of Art

PRINTER
Allied Printing

SEPARATOR
Carey Color

PAPER
**French Dur-o-tone, Proterra Flecks,
chipboard, wallpaper**

ENTRANT'S COMMENTS

I compensated for the lack of a guest speaker
for the college's Honors and Awards Night ceremony
by creating a story to entertain the audience.
The story began in the invitation. It revolves around
a character named Les trying to get a date for Honors
and Awards Night. Les is a real nerdy guy and he
keeps getting turned down. Out of desperation he
places an ad in the personals. The program is a
continuation of the story. Les sets up dates with
eight women who responded to his ad.

JUROR'S COMMENTS

This weird little booklet from Indiana uses thriftshop book board and sends its audience straight into the twilight
zone. **L.H.M.**

DESIGNER
Rebeca Méndez

CREATIVE DIRECTORS
Stuart I. Frolick, Rebeca Méndez

WRITERS
Edward A. Adams, David R. Brown

PHOTOGRAPHERS
Edward A. Adams, John D. Coleman,
George Jergenson and others

DESIGN FIRM
ACCD Design Office

CLIENT
Art Center College of Design

PRINTER/SEPARATOR
Typecraft Inc.

PAPER
Vintage Velvet, Caress, Ikonofix

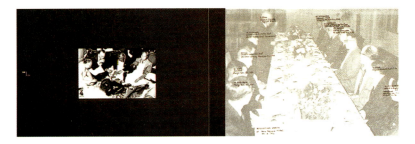

ENTRANT'S COMMENTS

The approach to the design of these pieces began
with an existing book, written and published in 1956
by Art Center's founder E.A. "Tink" Adams, which
was reproduced without any design alteration.
Its companion piece was designed around a set of
photographs made during Adams's trip to Japan.
The design suggests the intimate, personal quality of a
photo album. It also references the "archeology" of
these particular images, their discoloration with age,
and their markings, both intentional (handwritten
notes, rubber stamps, and reproduction codes) and
unintentional (tears, remnants of taped captions and
stains). The book honors the life recorded in the
images' content as well as the impact of time on
the photographs-as-objects.

JUROR'S COMMENTS

This beautifully packaged book is about one year in the life of a school. The designer shows a mastery of craft and
the concept of simplicity. **L.H.M.**

Jeff Corwin Photography

Promotion

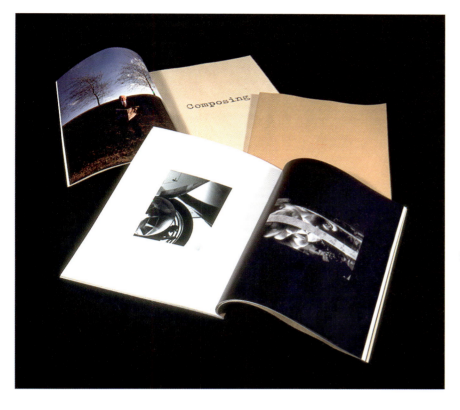

DESIGNERS
John Van Dyke, Ann Kumasaka

WRITER
Tom McCarthy

ART DIRECTOR
John Van Dyke

PHOTOGRAPHER
Jeff Corwin

DESIGN FIRM
Van Dyke Company

CLIENT
Jeff Corwin

PRINTER
H. MacDonald Printing

PAPER
**Eurocan cement bag liner, Mead Signature,
Aquabee Art Paper**

ENTRANT'S COMMENTS

As a recipient of many photographer promotions,
I considered myself typical of the audience for this
piece. It's a tough audience. We have seen it all:
cleverness, cuteness, overdesign and the occasional
piece that just works. The objective with the Corwin
piece was to simply place photo images in a framework
that would suggest a design context, along with a
simple use of copy sharing the photographer's
philosophy. The key to this piece is that you know
this is about photos and not about design.

JUROR'S COMMENTS

This piece expresses process as well as product. I like the brown wrap and the text. **L.H.M.**

DESIGNERS
Karen Salsgiver, Cathleen Mitchell

WRITERS
Karen Raven, Lynne Rutkin

CREATIVE DIRECTOR
Karen Salsgiver

DESIGN FIRM
**Salsgiver Coveney
Associates, Inc.**

CLIENT
The Juilliard School

PRINTER/SEPARATOR
Lebanon Valley Offset

PAPER
Champion Benefit and Kromekote

ENTRANT'S COMMENTS

This book is actually part two of a collaboration between The Juilliard School and Salsgiver Coveney Associates. We chose the slightly risky yet classic colors of Champion Benefit last year for Juilliard's first "real" annual report to serve as a metaphor for the philosophy and programs of the school. This year's report combines the same colors in a new format, a variation on a theme. The increments of change from year to year are subtle by design, with nuance meant to reflect the high level of the creative process at Juilliard.

JUROR'S COMMENTS

This piece has a sweet and tasteful feeling — thoughtful integrity, if not edibility. If the school is in a radical period, however, it's totally off! **L.H.M.**

Letterheads by
Fox River Paper Company

DESIGNERS
Steven Tolleson, Jennifer Sterling

ART DIRECTORS
Steven Tolleson, Jennifer Sterling

WRITER
Lindsay Beaman

DESIGN FIRM
Tolleson Design

CLIENT
Fox River Paper Company

PRINTER
Neenah Printing

PAPER
Confetti

ENTRANT'S COMMENTS

This piece was designed to showcase various business systems that had been designed on Confetti. An outer envelope is sealed on all four sides and contains the various systems. Business cards, envelopes and letterhead designs are graphically depicted while holes running along the top and bottom are incorporated to simulate the continuous feed forms that are an increasingly common element in corporate systems.

JUROR'S COMMENTS

The Confetti campaign is consistent, clean and clever. The typeface is like sharp-edged paper. **L.H.M.**

Mohawk Satin

DESIGNERS
Maria Grillo, Tim Bruce

WRITER
VSA Partners Inc.

ART DIRECTOR
Maria Grillo

PHOTOGRAPHER
Peter Frahm

DESIGN FIRM
VSA Partners, Inc.

CLIENT
Mohawk Paper Mills, Inc.

PRINTER
Columbia Graphics Corporation

PAPER
Mohawk Satin

ENTRANT'S COMMENTS

Mohawk Satin is an economically priced, laser-friendly smooth text and cover paper. This promotion is designed to present Mohawk Satin's new recycled colors to a diverse user audience — from quick printers to designers — for use on everything from flyers to financials. The piece focuses on the characteristics and uses of the paper in an accessible, informative and engaging manner while doubling as a counter card and hanging color chart.

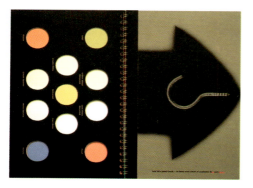

JUROR'S COMMENTS

Compared to many paper promotions, this is refreshingly downscale and simple; sensible for a laser-compatible paper promotion. L.H.M.

DESIGNERS
Jennifer Morla, Craig Bailey

PHOTOGRAPHER
Holly Stewart

DESIGN FIRM
Morla Design

CLIENT
San Francisco Airport Commission

TYPOGRAPHER
Morla Design

PRINTER/SEPARATOR
Fong & Fong

PAPER
Champion Benefit, Simpson Gainsborough

ENTRANT'S COMMENTS

The economic impact of SFIA to the Bay Area was the theme of its 1993 annual report. The key financial or quantititve figure found in each chapter is called out in order to show its importance. This is combined with a photographic visual that both illustrates the number/figure and relates to the subject of the chapter. The reader who quickly browses through the report will immediately understand the strong economic impact the airport has on both the Bay Area and Bay Area services.

JUROR'S COMMENTS

For an organization as massive as an airport, this is friendly, open and colorful. The essential material is **enhanced, not confused** by the additional graphics. **L.H.M.**

DESIGNERS
Somi Kim, Susan Parr, Lisa Nugent

WRITER
Carl Smith

ILLUSTRATOR
Chris Haaga

PHOTOGRAPHER
Paula Goldman

DESIGN FIRM
ReVerb, Los Angeles

CLIENT
Otis College of Art and Design

TYPOGRAPHERS
Somi Kim, Lisa Nugent, Susan Parr, Whitney Lowe

PRINTER/SEPARATOR
Frye & Smith

ENTRANT'S COMMENTS

The Otis poster visually pivots around the words "set things in motion" which has been the College's theme for recent recruitment materials. The image of the four winds blowing from the four corners of the world is inspired from 15th century European maps and is a concept most people are familiar with. We updated the image with photographs of students to add humor and believability to the underlying message that people initiate their future by today's actions. The poster is mailed to high schools and junior colleges to prompt inquiry.

JUROR'S COMMENTS

This poster illustrates the experience of graduate school: people blow in, create a centrifugal force, and the world spins wildly. The poster pulls the viewer in with incongruous elements being hurled everywhere. L.H.M.

Solid Waste

1992 Annual Report

DESIGNERS
Steve Pattee, Kelly Stiles

WRITER
Mike Condon

DESIGN FIRM
Pattee Design

CLIENT
Des Moines Metro Solid Waste Agency

PRINTER
Professional Offset

PAPER
Fox River Confetti, French Dur-o-tone

ENTRANT'S COMMENTS

The theme for this annual report communicates the need to do more than recycle. "Closing the Loop" brings together all the various ways we can reduce waste volume — the ultimate goal. The design solution was to make this report look and feel "found," as if it were made of various bits and pieces of paper found around the office. Camera-ready art was produced from laser-generated type and PMTs of Polaroids to give the piece a trashy feel.

JUROR'S COMMENTS

This piece has a clean and well-organized way of looking messy and deliberately chaotic. **L.H.M.**

Touch See

DESIGNERS
Curt Schreiber, Melissa Waters,
Ken Fox, Dana Arnett

WRITER
Nancy Lerner

ILLUSTRATOR
Bill Graham

PHOTOGRAPHER
Howard Bjornson

DESIGN FIRM
VSA Partners, Inc.

CLIENT
Potlatch Corporation

PRINTER/SEPARATOR
The Hennegan Company

PAPER
Potlatch Eloquence Silk

ENTRANT'S COMMENTS

This promotional book introduced a new silk surface
paper for Potlatch's premium grade Eloquence. The
book is divided into two sections, Touch and See. The
Touch section includes hands-on devices which allow
you to compare the surface of silk, gloss and other
paper finishes. The See section uses simple imagery
to compare the printing capabilities of Eloquence Silk
to those of other surfaces.

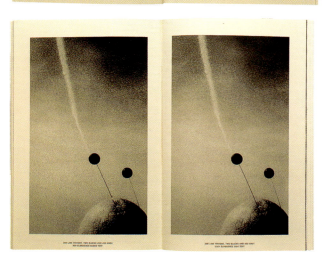

JUROR'S COMMENTS
This is a nice promotion that gives customers paper samples and little games to touch and see. L.H.M.

Wieland

Binder

DESIGNER
Neil Powell

WRITERS
John Jarvis, Chuck Carlson

PHOTOGRAPHERS
Mark LaFavor, Hugh Kretchsmer

DESIGN FIRM
Duffy Design

CLIENT
Wieland Furniture Company

PRINTER
Diversified Graphics

PAPER
French Dur-o-tone, Genuine Pressboard

ENTRANT'S COMMENTS

Wieland Furniture has been very successful in the health care and institutional markets. However, with the development of some new products, they felt it necessary to move into the architecture and design markets without disrupting their current customer base. This binder system is completely modular. With the use of metal tabs and an expandable binder, the sales representatives can easily customize presentations for any given client. The industrial construction of the catalog, along with its expandable quality, assures many years of service in the field.

JUROR'S COMMENTS

This is part of a very thorough image campaign. The binder's high level of construction detailing seems right for this furniture company. **L.H.M.**

DESIGNER
Neil Powell

DESIGN FIRM
Duffy Design

CLIENT
Wieland Furniture Company

PRINTER
Alternatives, Inc.

PAPER
French Dur-o-tone

ENTRANT'S COMMENTS

Wieland's repositioning from a manufacturer of
health care and institutional lounge seating
to a major player in the architecture and design
markets meant that they needed a corporate identity
system with sophistication coupled with visual impact.
We also needed to create an aesthetic which
would lend itself to the rest of the catalog system
we were designing. The linear chair pattern is
used as a backdrop which can be dialed up or down
with the use of color and composition.

JUROR'S COMMENTS

The **historical references** of the type are appropriate to the type of furniture this company makes.
The color combination is nice and chewy, with a smooth use of materials. **L.H.M.**

The **I O O** +2 show

Selections by:
Rudy VanderLans

Absolut

I.D. Campaign

DESIGNERS
Rick Valicenti, Mark Rattin

WRITER
Thirst

DIGITAL IMAGING
Mark Rattin, Rick Valicenti

DESIGN FIRM
Thirst

CLIENT
I.D. Magazine

TYPOGRAPHER
Thirst

ENTRANT'S COMMENTS

A specific audience: designers reading I.D. Magazine.
A discerning client: Michele Roux, Absolut Vodka.
A touch of pop and a Thirst sense of humor.

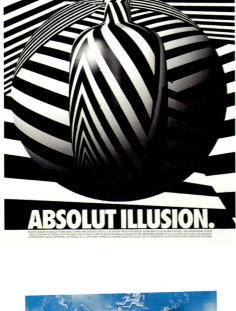

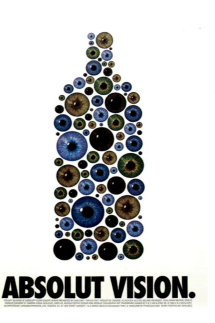

JUROR'S COMMENTS

One reason I picked this is because Rick was instrumental in getting this project off the ground. The designs are typical Thirst: a bit self-indulgent, full of visual/verbal puns and much technological magic and a little twisted. Yet Rick finds a place for these ideas within the mainstream by way of his entrepreneurial spirit. Instead of sitting back and moping about the conservatism and frugalness of clients, Rick is one of the few designers I know who often puts his money where his ideas are so to speak, to realize a project. And for that I respect him greatly. R.V.D.L.

ADCI

Call for Entries

DESIGNERS
Mario A. Mirelez, Jim Ross

WRITER
Jon A. Wagner

DESIGN FIRM
Mirelez/Ross Inc.

CLIENT
Art Directors Club of Indiana

TYPEFACE DESIGN
Edwin Utermohlen

PRINTER
Benham Press

PAPER
Strathmore Elements

ENTRANT'S COMMENTS

**The message is simple: enter the show and see
if you make the "cut."**

ADCI 94 *THE BEST SHOW*

CALL FOR ENTRIES

WHO IS ELIGIBLE TO ENTER?

ANY ART DIRECTOR, DESIGNER, WRITER, ILLUSTRATOR, PHOTOGRAPHER, STUDENT, ETC. WORKING ANYWHERE IN INDIANA.

WHAT ABOUT STUDENT ENTRIES?

THIS YEAR, INDIANA STUDENTS MAY CHOOSE TO ENTER EITHER AS REGULAR ENTRANTS OR IN THE STUDENT DIVISION. OR, DOUBLE YOUR PLEASURE BY ENTERING IN BOTH! YOU MUST, HOWEVER, SUBMIT TWO SEPARATE COPIES OF YOUR WORK, TWO SEPARATE ENTRY FORMS, AND TWO—TWO ENTRY FEES(!) QUALIFY AS A STUDENT ENTRY, YOUR WORK DOESN'T NECESSARILY HAVE TO BE PUBLISHED OR PROFESSIONALLY PRINTED—JUST PRODUCED BY YOU BETWEEN THE DATES ELIGIBLE. PLEASE ATTACH A PHOTOCOPY OF YOUR STUDENT I.D. OR OTHER FORM OF CONFIRMATION FOR THE 1993-94 SCHOOL YEAR.

WHAT IS ELIGIBLE?

ANY PRINT OR BROADCAST COMMUNICATION PUBLISHED OR APPEARING BETWEEN THE 1ST OF MAY, 1993 THROUGH THE 1ST OF MAY, 1994. THIS INCLUDES ADVERTISING, PROMOTION, ANNUAL REPORTS AND OTHER CORPORATE PUBLICATIONS, POSTERS, MAGAZINES, NEWSPAPERS, BOOK COVERS, CD AND RECORD COVERS, LOGOS AND SYMBOLS, LETTERHEADS, MENUS, CALENDARS, PACKAGING, BILLBOARDS, RADIO SPOTS, TV COMMERCIAL SALES VIDEOS, SCRIPTS, ETC.

HOW SHOULD ENTRIES BE PREPARED?

PRINT: MOUNT PRINT ENTRIES ON 15" X 20" OR 20" X 30" BLACK MAT BOARD.

UN-MOUNTABLE ENTRIES: SUBMIT AN 8" X 10" COLOR PHOTOGRAPH MOUNTED ON A 15" X 20" BLACK MAT BOARD FOR LARGE, BULKY OR ON-LOCATION ENTRIES THAT CANNOT BE MOUNTED (SUCH AS BILLBOARDS, SIGNAGE, PACKAGING, ETC.).

MULTIPLE BOARDS: SINGLE ENTRIES USING MULTIPLE BOARDS SHOULD BE HINGED WITH BLACK TAPE.

BROADCAST: SUBMIT TELEVISION ENTRIES ON 3/4" CASSETTE—NO BLANKS, COLOR BARS OR TONES. LABEL CASSETTES AND RECORD MULTIPLE ENTRIES BACK-TO-BACK. SUBMIT RADIO ENTRIES ON A LABELED AUDIO CASSETTE. ALL BROADCAST ENTRIES SHOULD BE ACCOMPANIED BY A SCRIPT.

HOW MUCH DOES IT COST TO ENTER?

EACH ENTRY:	CAMPAIGN FEES:
(SINGLE ENTRY)	(THREE OR MORE RELATED WORKS)
$20 MEMBERS	$30 MEMBERS
$30 NON-MEMBERS	$40 NON-MEMBERS
$10 STUDENT MEMBERS	$15 STUDENT MEMBERS
$20 STUDENT NON-MEMBERS	$25 STUDENT NON-MEMBERS

WHAT SHOULD ACCOMPANY ENTRIES?

AN ENTRY FORM (SEE ATTACHED) MUST BE TAPED OR GLUED—NO STAPLES OR PAPER CLIPS, PLEASE—TO THE BACK UPPER RIGHT-HAND CORNER OF EACH ENTRY SUBMITTED. EACH PIECE IN A CAMPAIGN OR SERIES MUST HAVE AN ENTRY FORM (THUS A THREE-PART AD CAMPAIGN MUST HAVE THREE FORMS). PLEASE TYPE OR PRINT CLEARLY ON EACH ENTRY FORM AS COMPLETELY AND ACCURATELY AS POSSIBLE.

AN OBJECTIVE STATEMENT (ATTACHED/OPTIONAL) MAY BE TAPED TO THE RIGHT UPPER RIGHT-HAND CORNER OF EACH BOARD.

A MASTER LIST (ENCLOSED) OF ALL ENTRIES SUBMITTED BY THE ENTRANT (CORPORATION OR INDIVIDUAL) MUST BE INCLUDED ALONG WITH THE ENTRIES AND ENTRY FEE.

YOUR PAYMENT: MUST BE ENCLOSED WITH EACH PACKAGE OF ENTRIES. MAKE CHECKS PAYABLE TO: ART DIRECTORS CLUB OF INDIANA. ENTRIES WITHOUT PAYMENT WILL NOT BE CONSIDERED.

WHAT IS THE DEADLINE?

ENTRIES MUST BE DELIVERED IN PERSON OR VIA COURIER BETWEEN 10:00 A.M. & 5:00 PM., FRIDAY THE 10TH OF JUNE TO: NORMAN'S AT UNION STATION (EVENING), 39W. JACKSON PLACE (SOUTH DRIVE), DOWNTOWN INDIANAPOLIS. A LATE FEE OF $10 PER ENTRY MUST BE INCLUDED WITH ALL ENTRIES RECEIVED BETWEEN 5:00 P.M. AND 9:00 P.M., FRIDAY THE 10TH OF JUNE. NO ENTRIES WILL BE ACCEPTED AFTER 9:00 P.M. ENTRIES COMING VIA MAIL, SERVICE MUST BE RECEIVED BY JUNE 9, 1994 AND ADDRESSED TO: RIS STUDIOS, INC. C/O RICHARD SPENCER 615 NORTH ALABAMA, INDIANAPOLIS, INDIANA 46202.

WHAT ELSE SHOULD I KNOW?

SORRY, BUT ENTRIES TO THE ADCI BEST SHOW CANNOT BE RETURNED. IF YOU ARE SUBMITTING A ONE-OF-A-KIND PIECE AND WOULD LIKE IT BACK, PLEASE MAKE ARRANGEMENTS THROUGH RICHARD SPENCER.

AND NOW, THE FINE PRINT: ...

IF YOU HAVE ANY QUESTIONS, PLEASE CALL RICHARD SPENCER AT (317) 206-4586.

DESIGN: MIRELEZ/ROSS INC.
WRITER: JON A. WAGNER
TYPEFACE: RIS E'S USED TYPE BY EDWIN UTERMOHLEN
TYPE OUTPUT: TRIPLE J TYPOGRAPHERS
PAPER: STRATHMORE ELEMENTS: SOFT GRAY LINES, DOTS & SQUARES

RIS|SOURCE

JUROR'S COMMENTS

I was particularly attracted to the typography on the back of this poster. It's clumsy but powerful, and upon closer examination there are many typographic details showing us that this wasn't exactly one big accident. It has attained typographic "color" in a rather unusual way. It's obvious to me that this is done with as much intent as is, let's say, Steve Tolleson's perfectly executed Radius Annual Report. **R.V.D.L.**

AIGA/Raleigh Cigarette

Poster

DESIGNER
Paula Scher

PHOTOGRAPHER
John Paul Endress

DESIGN FIRM
Pentagram

CLIENT
AIGA/Raleigh

TYPOGRAPHERS
Paula Scher, Ron Louie

PRINTER
Teagle & Little

PAPER
Finch Fine Smooth

ENTRANT'S COMMENTS

This is a poster for a talk I gave in Raleigh, North Carolina, the heart of tobacco country. I smoke Parliaments.

WARNING: Paula Scher in Raleigh
Presented by AIGA, Sponsored by FGI
Thursday, February 24, 1994, 7:30pm
100 Hamilton Hall, University of
North Carolina, Chapel Hill

JUROR'S COMMENTS

As an early fan of the New York school of "ideas-based" graphics, I really enjoy this poster. It's this type of work that turned me on to graphic design. Very direct, powerful and understood by everybody. If this is the age of pluralism, then there definitely should be a place for this. It makes me wonder how dangerous Paula thinks she really is. But I guess that's why it's such a good poster. R.V.D.L.

Al Held Italian Watercolors

DESIGNER
Renate Gokl

WRITER
Maarten van de Guchte

CLIENT
Krannert Art Museum

TYPOGRAPHER
Renate Gokl

PRINTER
**University of Illinois
Office of Printing Services**

SEPARATOR
Flying Color Graphics

PAPER
**Gilbert Esse, Simpson Evergreen,
Hammermill Opaque**

ENTRANT'S COMMENTS

In short, form supports content. The objective
of this exhibition catalog was to capture the spirit
of Held's watercolors without emulating them
or detracting from them. The catalog was to provide
a backdrop with which to view the work and
which functioned to reinforce ideas inherent in
Held's paintings, such as plays on perspective,
classic proportions and spatial illusions.
The layout provides a field where the interaction
of image and text is integral and allows one to
make visual relationships and connections.
One might begin to question where the physical
realm of the painting actually ends. The interviews
are treated in a way which maintains the energy
and enthusiasm that occurred between the artist and
his interviewer — a flow, sensitive to the dynamics
of these conversations. Reading becomes an act
of listening, hearing, imagination and involvement.

JUROR'S COMMENTS

This is not breaking any new ground, although I was attracted to the delicately animated way the interview in the
back was treated. Otherwise, this is a quiet, stylish catalog. Perhaps I picked this because it is representative of a
large number of submissions that were of high quality that I feel get overlooked due to the visual overload
of the entire show. R.V.D.L.

Art Center at Night

DESIGNER
Darin Beaman

WRITER
Sarah Russin

PHOTOGRAPHER
Steven A. Heller

DESIGN FIRM
ACCD Design Office

CLIENT
Art Center College of Design

PRINTER/SEPARATOR
Typecraft Inc.

PAPER
Recovery Matte Book

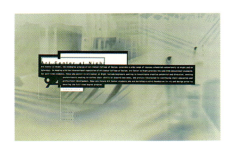

ENTRANT'S COMMENTS

The abstract photographic treatment in this brochure for Art Center's night program was inspired by the optical phenomenon of the afterimage. These pictures were created at night by shooting multiple exposures with fixed focus cameras and then utilizing both negative and positive imagery. The "no-frills" utilitarian typeface Letter Gothic was chosen to contrast the dark moody open spaces of shadow and light that give Art Center's distinctive architecture a nighttime character all its own.

JUROR'S COMMENTS

Simple and elegant, with great use of photography. There's a consistency to the quality of the work coming out of the Art Center design office that is quite remarkable. And there's a sensitivity at play that makes the work immediately recognizable without having an obvious unifying house identity. **R.V.D.L.**

DESIGNER
Susan Lally

WRITERS
Harry Wirth and the featured designers

PHOTOGRAPHERS
Harry Wirth, Susan Lally and others

DESIGN FIRM
Lally Design

PUBLISHER
Harry J. Wirth/The American Design Network

TYPOGRAPHER
Susan Lally

PRINTER
Bulfin Printers

PAPER
Mohawk Superfine and Satin

ENTRANT'S COMMENTS

In expressing the objective of the Art of Design 2
exhibition, I designed the museum catalog to celebrate
the range of content and voices in American design.
The ambiguous nature of the creative process is given
the same importance as the clarity of the designer's
philosophies and finished work. In structuring
and pacing the pages of the book, my goal was to
respect and reflect the full range of rhythms, as
the viewer would, in exploring and experiencing
the exhibition. The book's pacing changes from
subtle differences between elements to dramatic
juxtapositions to create a visual richness paralleling
the eclectic in American design.

JUROR'S COMMENTS

The designer obviously didn't go easy on herself. Typographically it's an overwhelming effort, and the result is a
catalog brimming with activity and allure. I enjoy the fact that it allows you to enter at any point,
much like the way I enjoy looking at exhibitions. All that, and a considerate use of resources as well. I tip my hat.
R.V.D.L.

DESIGNERS
Peter King Robbins, Neville Burtis

WRITER
Tabitha De La Torre

PHOTOGRAPHERS
Amedeo, Glen Erler

DESIGN FIRM
BRD Design, Inc.

ENTRANT'S COMMENTS

Spare graphics and sensual photography were combined to convey both the corporate nature of our business and the spiritual side of the creative process. The use of bird imagery reinforces our pronunciation of our studio's name. Our annual calendar allows us an opportunity to take chances with design. Through the calendar's theme, everyday life, we tried to retain playfulness in the design and photography as well as in the text. In our promotion we contrasted the clean presentation of our work with the organic nature of the handmade cover stock and the natural corrugated cardboard case.

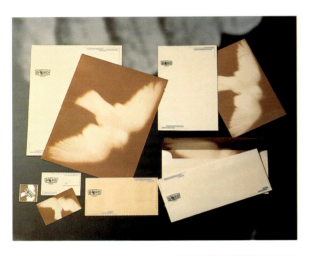

JUROR'S COMMENTS

This just looks so damn inevitable. A calendar as a capabilities piece is a great idea. **R.V.D.L.**

DESIGNER
Elliott Earls

WRITER
Elliott Earls

ILLUSTRATOR
Elliott Earls

TYPOGRAPHER
Elliott Earls

PRINTER
American Graphics

SEPARATOR
Typogram

PAPER
Mohawk Vellum

ENTRANT'S COMMENTS

It was conceived deep within the "Mr. Plastic Hair." It is words, that sieve, that fatty sandwich of slipped meaning, of misfired synapse. A gauze sinew, holding fast the grey slunk-meat substance on life's most favored vacuum formed sandwich. (Ideas) Churned out like so many shiny new salisbury steaks from agri-business factories somewhere in the golden bosom of industrial New Jersey. With gleaming heart, pumping and bumping to the syncopated rhythm of office boys chanting the mantra: "We desire plain and simple charity." Well I ain't your boy. And so, the question becomes, "Why speak English when you can get paid to speak gibberish?" Ah, gibberish, the language of kings. How do I love thee? This gibberish (this question) goads me, prods and pokes me. Dare I say consumes me? It is therein I jabber endlessly, saying nothing, and meaning every word of it.

JUROR'S COMMENTS

Like Rick Valicenti, Elliott Earls has a knack for creating a ready-made context for his bizarre type designs to exist in. To me Elliott Earls, by making new and unusual typefaces appear far more usable than they might actually be, is the Herb Lubalin of our time. It's also encouraging to see that more designers are initiating their own projects instead of waiting for that "perfect" client to call. R.V.D.L.

DESIGNERS
Rick Valicenti, Mark Rattin

WRITERS
Various

ILLUSTRATORS
Mark Rattin, Rick Valicenti

DESIGN FIRM
Thirst

CLIENT
Arts Club of Chicago

TYPOGRAPHERS
Mark Rattin, Rick Valicenti

PRINTER
Universal

PAPER
French Speckletone

JUROR'S COMMENTS

This booklet is **probably too "designed" by Fluxus standards,** which brings up the question of whether the design of art catalogs should reflect the art shown or be subservient and let the art speak for itself. This catalog seems to do a little of both. The text is relatively straightforward without being predictable, while some parts of the catalog pay tribute to Fluxus ideologies such as collectivism, which is nicely illustrated on the cover, and anti-establishmentism, demonstrated through the use of cheap paper and simple black and white reproductions. **R.V.D.L.**

Fluxus

Poster

DESIGNERS
Rick Valicenti, Mark Rattin

DIGITAL IMAGING
Rick Valicenti, Mark Rattin

DESIGN FIRM
Thirst

CLIENT
Arts Club of Chicago

TYPOGRAPHERS
Mark Rattin, Rick Valicenti

PRINTER
Carqueville/TCR Graphics

ENTRANT'S COMMENTS

This poster was posted publicly during Fluxus month in Chicago. It was also folded and mailed to the Arts Club membership. From a communication point of view, it asks what is funny, legible, beautiful, appropriate, etc. All rendering was in the spirit, not the style, of Fluxus.

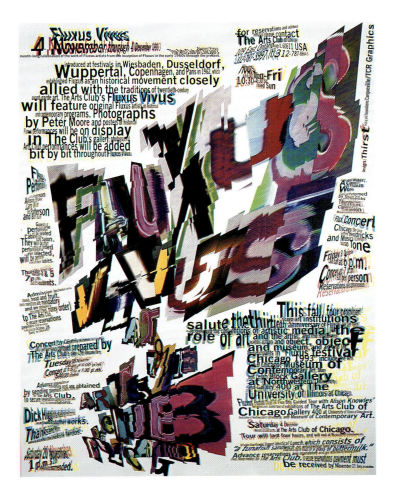

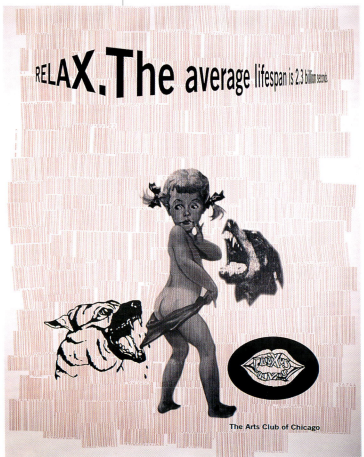

JUROR'S COMMENTS

Here the connection with Fluxus is nearly nonexistent, but in its place we have an incredibly powerful, loud and hard to ignore poster which brings attention to a group of artists who were fairly underground and nearly overlooked because of it. Perhaps they deserve a gutsy poster like this. **R.V.D.L.**

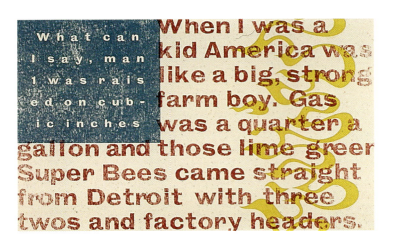

DESIGNER
Bob Dahlquist

WRITER
Bob Dahlquist

ILLUSTRATOR
Bob Dahlquist

DESIGN FIRM
Bob's Haus

CLIENT
Bob's Haus

TYPOGRAPHER
Bob Dahlquist

PRINTER
Tom's Printing, Inc.

PAPER
Fox River Circa

ENTRANT'S COMMENTS

My ode to American innocence. I was 12 years old in 1969 and Detroit was king, building big, garish muscle cars. The rowdy neighbor kid across the street was raising hell with his friend, who actually had one of those Dodge Super Bees. A couple years later, after serving his time in Viet Nam, he came home and commited suicide. So this flag's a little beat up and showing some wear. (The rough texture was achieved on press, by backing off the pressure between the blanket and impression cylinders.) The hot rod flames are there as a nod to 1960s exuberance...or is the flag burning?

JUROR'S COMMENTS

I love this for its language, its typeface and its wood block printing quality. I'm partial to it as a foreigner because this is what makes America such a fantastically romantic place. Where else do people have love relationships with carburetors? R.V.D.L.

DESIGNER
Rosanne Lobes

CURATOR
Mitchell Kane

CATALOG CONCEPT
Mitchell Kane, Rosanne Lobes

DESIGN FIRM
Maginnis Inc.

CLIENT
Hirsch Farm Project

PRINTER/SEPARATOR
Production Press

PAPER
Swan, Strathmore Writing

ENTRANT'S COMMENTS

This book documents the proposals, support literature and photography of last year's Hirsch Farm Project, an arts-based think tank located in Hillsboro, Wisconsin. The design intent was to provide a flexible, cohesive structure for the wildly diverse documentation; to meet the curator's request for a practical, unselfconscious, simple solution, and to reflect the book's title and theme: "Nonspectacle and the Limitations of Popular Opinion." I tried to use subtle, unexpected shifts and twists which call into question popular assumptions about book format. I wanted the cover and global design treatment to be quiet and "nonspectacular," and the completed book, through its intelligence, its heart and its nuance, to feel special and memorable.

JUROR'S COMMENTS

Talk about non-spectacle! I picked this purely for its cover design. What restraint! The inside turned out to be a handsome bonus as well. **R.V.D.L.**

DESIGNER
Anita Meyer

WRITER AND CURATOR
Judith Hoos Fox

COVER DESIGN
Annette Lemieux

PHOTOGRAPHERS
Eric Shambroom, Ellen Page Wilson

PRODUCTION COORDINATOR
Susan McNally

DESIGN FIRM
plus design inc.

CLIENT
Davis Museum and Cultural Center

TYPOGRAPHY
Moveable Type Inc.

PRINTER
Meridian Printing Company

PAPER
French Dur-o-tone

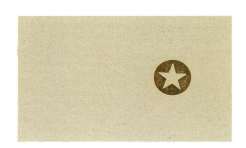

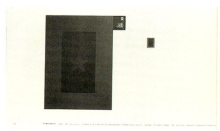 

ENTRANT'S COMMENTS

This catalog accompanies an exhibition of the work of noted contemporary artist Annette Lemieux. Working closely with Lemieux, plus drew from recurrent themes in her work, interruption and repetition, which suggested a design for the catalog. The typography, visual and conceptual interruptions, newsprint stock and star image branded by the artist on the cover, all derive from the artist's work. This publication not only documents the exhibition but expresses the means and content of Lemieux's work.

JUROR'S COMMENTS

The star in a circle, emblazoned on American military vehicles, is a great signifier for the end of the Second World War, particularly since that war was dominated by another emblem: the swastika. I didn't immediately understand the meaning of the graphic on the cover until I flipped through the catalog. When I made the connection, however, I couldn't help but think what a brilliant design it was, although I'm not sure if my interpretation is entirely right.
R.V.D.L.

New Order "Republic"

Special Package

DESIGNERS
Peter Saville, Brett Wickens

ART DIRECTION
Jeff Gold, Peter Saville, Steven Baker

DESIGN FIRM
Pentagram

CLIENT
Qwest/Warner Bros. Records

TYPOGRAPHER
Pentagram

PRINTER
Ivy Hill

SEPARATOR
Color Service, Inc.

PAPER
Kimdura

ENTRANT'S COMMENTS

The album cover featured a couple playing tug of war with an inflatable innertube. We thought this was a great jumping off point for a special package, and decided we would do something with vinyl innertube material of the same color. When we saw the first sample we decided it was a bit "flat" and that we should try to "inflate" it. I thought of the plastic books my young daughters played with in the bathtub, and voila; everything came together. To make the whole thing "bathtub safe" we printed the booklet on very thin vinyl instead of paper. And the best part: it floats!

JUROR'S COMMENTS

I can't help looking at this limited edition CD without thinking of all the other pieces that make up the package for this release by New Order. It's the most persuasive music packaging I've seen recently. The designer working in the world of contemporary rock music should be given a bit of creative license, allowing for exploration and some self-indulgence. Peter Saville has attained that status, yet he never misuses that privilege. His work is always intelligent. **R.V.D.L.**

OK

Cans

DESIGNER
Todd Waterbury

WRITER
Peter Wegner

ILLUSTRATORS
Calef Brown, Charles Burns,
Daniel Clowes, Todd Waterbury

DESIGN FIRM
Wieden & Kennedy

CLIENT
The Coca-Cola Company

TYPOGRAPHER
Todd Waterbury

PRINTER
Crown Cork and Seal

ENTRANT'S COMMENTS

The OK Manifesto: 1. What's the point of "OK"? Well, what's the point of anything? 2. "OK" emphatically rejects anything that is not OK, and fully supports anything that is. 3. The better you understand something, the more OK it turns out to be. 4. "OK" soda says, "Don't be fooled into thinking there has to be a reason for everything." 5. "OK" reveals the surprising truth about people and situations. 6. "OK" does not subscribe to any religion, or endorse any political party, or do anything other than feel OK. 7. "There is no real secret to feeling OK." Attributed to "OK" soda, 1997. 8. "OK" may be the preferred drink of other people such as yourself. 9. Never underestimate the remarkable abilities of "OK" brand soda.

JUROR'S COMMENTS

This is about as bold a step as one can take in the world of beverage packaging. It addresses its intended audience in a language they understand and enjoy. Perhaps the biggest obstacle to its success is the fact that it is produced by Coca-Cola, a fact that is visible in the credit line. The audience might just feel that OK is not as spontaneous and innocent as it aspires to be. On the other hand, if Generation X will swallow Beck, I don't see why they wouldn't buy into this. R.V.D.L.

Paul Westerberg "14 Songs"

Special Package

ART DIRECTION
Kim Champagne, Jeff Gold

CONCEPT AND DESIGN
Paul Westerberg, Kim Champagne

BOOKLET DESIGN
Kim Champagne, Jean Krikorian

PHOTOGRAPHERS
Frank Ockenfels, Kim Champagne

DESIGN FIRM
Warner Bros. Records

CLIENT
Reprise/Sire Records

PRINTER
Ivy Hill

SEPARATOR
Color Inc.

PAPER
Chipboard, Williamsburg Hi-bulk, Kraft, Grandee

ENTRANT'S COMMENTS

This special package was fun to put together.
Everything was done very quickly. By the time
deadlines and prices had been established we were
close to missing our due dates. The cover for the
book was due first. It was made to look like the book
Paul is holding on the front of the regular CD package.
Colors and materials were meant to be simple and
humble. The inside contains an interview by
Bill Bentley and some great photos of Paul we did not
get to use earlier. Jean Krikorian did a lovely job
designing the inside. Obviously, the idea was to make
this look as much like a real book as possible.
I think we were successful.

JUROR'S COMMENTS

This is a **curiously quiet** package for an artist who's known to go on an occasional rampage on stage. However, with his band The Replacements no longer in existence, and the fact that Westerberg is now considered somewhat of a rock and roll classic, perhaps this **reflective, traditional** approach is fitting, although it's a bit sad as well. In that respect I'm not sure if this design "solved the problem" or did justice to Westerberg, but it did make me curious. And the contrast between the traditional letterpress-inspired design and rock and roll is electrifying. **R.V.D.L.**

DESIGNER
Greg Lindy

ART DIRECTOR
Michael G. Rey

DESIGN FIRM
REY International

PRINTER
Stacey Hauge Printing

PAPER
Simpson Evergreen

ENTRANT'S COMMENTS

The poster is the REY International's 1994 greeting for the new year. It is designed to be a multi-level puzzle posing questions and odd relationships. There is no one way to look at the poster and the viewer is asked to arrive at his or her own conclusions. The main idea was to create something fun and to ask the question, "What's a waggle?"

JUROR'S COMMENTS

I've had this in my office for a while and I'm still trying to figure out what it means. I can't dismiss it simply because I don't understand it, because formally it's very attractive. It gives me so many layers of information; I'm still trying to add it all up and expect some kind of meaningful narrative to surface. I know it's a self-promotional piece so, to an extent, it's already served its purpose. But maybe there's an additional message that I'll eventually find. If in the end I find out it means nothing, we'll come and take the award back. R.V.D.L.

DESIGNER
Michael Bierut

ILLUSTRATOR
Reven T.C. Wurman

DESIGN FIRM
Pentagram

CLIENT
**Goddard Riverside
Community Center**

PRINTER
Ambassador Arts

ENTRANT'S COMMENTS

This poster announces a book fair sponsored by the
Goddard Riverside Community Center and the New York
publishing community. It was really easy to do.

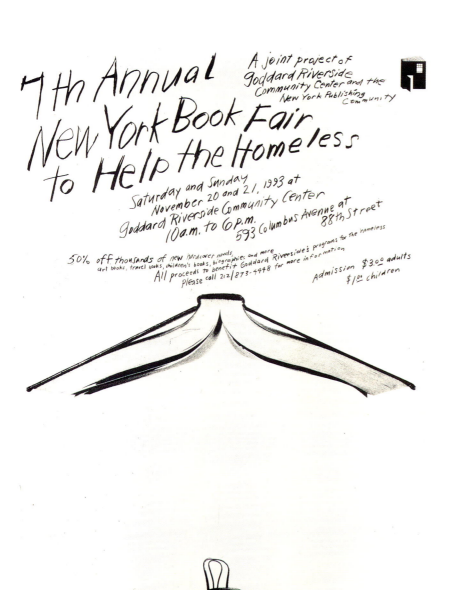

JUROR'S COMMENTS

This is a solid idea, modestly produced, for a worthy cause. That's good enough for me. **R.V.D.L.**

DESIGNER
Nan Goggin

CURATOR
Maarten van de Guchte

ILLUSTRATOR
Gam Klutier

CLIENT
Krannert Art Museum and Kinkead Pavilion,
University of Illinois at Champaign

TYPOGRAPHER
Nan Goggin

PRINTER
University of Illinois Office of Printing

PAPER
Simpson Evergreen

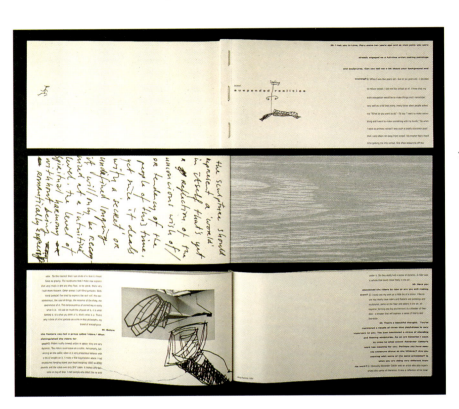

ENTRANT'S COMMENTS

The opened 21" by 5.5" dimensions were inspired by the Dutch artist's large horizontal, raw wood and metal sculptures that are precariously suspended from the ceiling. The 34-page booklet was produced entirely on the computer, with a low budget and a good sense of humor from the printer, with the spec'd requirement of "big honk" in silver staples. A running dialog begins on the cover and continues throughout the outer edges of the catalog. Interspersed on the pages are drawings from the artist's sketchbooks placed in relation to the sculptures.

JUROR'S COMMENTS

I like it because it is simple and unpretentious, yet sufficiently elegant and effective. **R.V.D.L.**

DESIGNER
Martin Venezky

WRITER
Martin Venezky

DESIGN FIRM
Studio Dumbar

CLIENT
Theater Zeebelt

TYPOGRAPHER
Martin Venezky

ENTRANT'S COMMENTS

Zeebelt is a Dutch experimental theater, and this postcard solicits members to keep the theater running. The card's modesty belies the importance of its task, and so began my investigation. Pondering how the minute can encompass the gigantic, I pieced small typographic slivers into full words, then chose four words, "surrender wealth, occupy myth," to describe how and why a community supports the arts. Finally, two photographs discovered in a flea market tenderly suggest how the simplest gesture — a dog turning on a woman's lap, her body mimicking the motion — could echo as an infinite moment of theater itself.

JUROR'S COMMENTS

Sometimes a certain image and word combination can just hook itself into your brain, like a few bars of a song, and won't let go. This is just a simple subscription drive postcard, but leave it to the Dutch to not let any design opportunity go wasted. I don't really know why I like this so much, it's just that I can't get that little dog out of my head. **R.V.D.L.**

Wieland

Capabilities Brochure

DESIGNER
Neil Powell

WRITER
John Jarvis

PHOTOGRAPHERS
Mark LaFavor, Hugh Kretchsmer

DESIGN FIRM
Duffy Design

CLIENT
Wieland Furniture Company

PRINTER
Diversified Graphics

PAPER
Centura Dull

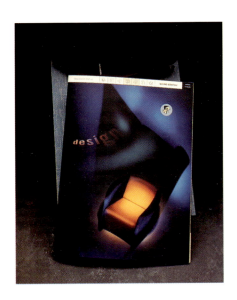

ENTRANT'S COMMENTS

We set out to create a capabilities brochure that would infuse Wieland's manufacturing capabilities with their business philosophy. With the use of Hugh Kretchsmer's and Mark LaFavor's photography, we not only told the story of how the furniture is made, but maybe more importantly, why it was made.

JUROR'S COMMENTS

It's all so silky smooth and streamlined and 1950s looking — except in the 1950s they didn't have such exquisite photo reproduction and printing technologies available. I'm not sure if I'm in awe or simply intimidated by the quality of the pieces that make up the identity for Wieland. It would be easy to dismiss the work because of its flaunted luxuriousness and questionable use of resources. But if we're going to use up resources, we might as well dress them up best we can. There's a printer out there who is probably pretty proud of what they accomplished, as well they should be. I wonder if Duffy files his awards alphabetically, or whether there's room left on the walls in his office. **R.V.D.L.**

DESIGNERS
Neil Powell, Kobe, Jeff Johnson, Alan Leusink

ILLUSTRATORS
Neil Powell, Kobe, Jeff Johnson, Alan Leusink

DESIGN FIRM
Duffy Design

CLIENT
World Conservation Poster

PAPER
Mohawk Superfine

ENTRANT'S COMMENTS

We like to build things.

JUROR'S COMMENTS

Nothing beats hand-drawn illustrations to show human effort. Humanitarian and environmental causes such as this are well served by such an approach. **R.V.D.L.**

Yoko Ono

Catalog/Poster

DESIGNER
Fred Bower

WRITER
Yoko Ono

PHOTOGRAPHERS
Karla Merrifield, Lenono,
David Behl, William Nettles,
George Marcuinas, Adam Reich

CLIENTS
Yoko Ono, Cranbrook Academy of Art

PRINTER
Great Lakes

ENTRANT'S COMMENTS

The reason for packaging a catalog and a poster together was primarily to save money. They wanted a catalog and poster (among other things) but didn't want to put up the dough. Okay... Otherwise I just wanted a nice, clean, elegant, typographic piece.

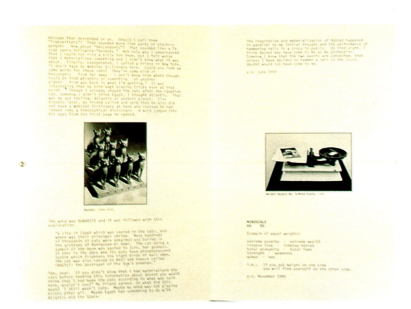

JUROR'S COMMENTS

This has a rather unique and personal quality to it attained with limited means. It's very quiet, yet bold in its curious mix of typefaces, and thoughtful in how it functions as both a booklet and a small poster. **R.V.D.L.**

Product Design Year

in Review

Essays by

Bill Moggridge

R. Craig Miller

Bruce Sterling

What's **Happening?**

Bill Moggridge

We're going soft

In 1981 I spent two weeks in North Carolina on a MacAuto training course, learning to drive our first engineering CAD system. At that time I still made a point of personally learning how to use all the tools of our trade so that I could talk shop with anyone in our design team. Before that I had usually learned how to do physical things like driving a milling machine or using an airbrush, but this was a new virtual world and a precedent for the soft invasion. Now, fourteen years later, computerized tools have driven a wedge between me and my friends; I'm hopelessly behind almost everyone in the company. I haven't learned the simple CAD used by our industrial designers, let alone the solid modeler used by the engineers; I can't use the illustration packages that have replaced magic markers, let alone the Alias visualization system, nor can I script Macromedia Director to simulate interactive solutions, nor program the NC milling machines or run a finite element analysis. Every year I take my computer with me on vacation and teach myself to use a new tool, but the expertise I gain in the ten hours devoted to the exercise is not enough to let me talk shop intelligently; it just makes me admire the accomplishment of my colleagues who have real fluency and understanding of the kit of soft tools that they use.

   Computerized tools have turned us into softies and the big bang is driving us apart, so that working together remains the biggest challenge that we face.

The big bang theory of design
Illustrated by Philip Davies of IDEO

We're flying apart

Here's a sketch of design's big bang in progress. All these different sorts of designers have to work together on the same product. You can see who's who by the shape of their heads; the software engineer is a floppy disc, the industrial designer a pencil, hardware designer a chip, interaction designer a monitor, and so on. They may be making some effort to understand each other but it sometimes seems like they are only succeeding in misunderstanding each other; they attend cross-functional team meetings on a regular schedule approved by the current version of the quality development process, but this doesn't get them to really work together. The problem is that they are being propelled apart by the force of the big bang explosion faster than they can get used to each other.

   Specialist expertise is harder to keep pace with as each discipline becomes more sophisticated, making each skill narrower and more focused. Good-bye renaissance designer; good-bye the days when one designer could do it all, taking credit for the complete authorship of a whole product. Now we're always working together in a team, multi-disciplinary parallel developers, struggling to stay expert at our own bit without losing touch with our colleagues in the discipline next door.

Bill Moggridge

We're all over the place

When you call an operator in the U.S. from some far off land, you are likely to talk to someone who is working at home. Steve MacDonald writes a column about design in *The Wall Street Journal*, working from his home in upstate New York. A mother of three verifies credit cards for a living, stepping into the on-line corner of the living room to log on; if a child needs attention she leaves work for a while. Marshall McLuhan's Global Village seems to be real at last, triggered by the falling cost of electronic equipment and communications.

Driven by the Clean Air Act, New Jersey will introduce a new law next year requiring a 20% reduction in the number of cars on the road, mandating employers to conform. As a result companies are asking employees to work at home, providing them with an allowance to furnish a part of their home like an office. This change comes from Congress, but companies are going along with it ahead of time because they can see potential reductions in the cost of facilities. If people work at home enough to share office space, fewer offices are needed.

As design is full of independent minded people who revel in beautiful places, perhaps we will welcome physical separation, as the technology of communications allows us to work in places that we like. Those people who spend too long on airplanes will like the idea of reducing the need for travel.

What makes a design significant?

It is designed with people in mind.

It knows its audience. It is designed for you, and especially you. It is not just for the designer and friends. It shows that it knows about the whole range of people who use it. Not the average, but the whole range, from the slowest to the quickest or the oldest to the youngest.

It fulfills a dream.

What about the fantasy? Where are the dreams? A significant design delivers some magic; some combination of beauty of form, a balanced synthesis of elegance, an ingenious solution, a delight to use, a multisensory combination of appearance, touch and sound.

It shows the way.

Significance implies discovery. Perhaps it's an innovative design or a new way of doing it. It sets a precedent.

Something excellent.

The beholder will spontaneously exclaim "ah-ha" or some other expression of admiration or wonder, as they realize the excellence of some feature or quality of the design.

Two Aeron chairs from Herman Miller
Designed by Don Chadwick and Bill Stumpf

Hard with Soft: The Aeron Chair

The new range of office chairs from Herman Miller designed by Bill Stumpf and Don Chadwick combines a hard looking new material with a delectably soft and comfortable feel.

It looks hard, dark and technical with mechanical sinews stretching out from the sump of a block of gears that floats eerily in mid air. The exoskeleton of monocoque framework surrounding seat and back has an insect-like blend of structural tension and organic grace. The appearance repels, and at the same time engages, making you want to come closer to feel and try, but warily as if approaching a machine that could be aggressive rather than supportive.

The surface of seat and back must be touched first in order to resolve the conflict between the mind saying that the material must be soft and comfortable, but the eye recoiling with the certainty that it is a finely woven chain mail, suitable perhaps for protecting police officers from bullets, but not for sitting on. Close your eyes and touch it and your mind jeers "told you so!" as the supple yet firm sensuality immediately proves comfort, but with eyes open it is still surprising to see the ease with which the surface deforms.

The Aeron chair - front view

The Pellicle

Sample screen from multimedia presentation. Designed by Clement Mok

Hardware with Software.

The Aeron chair is so strongly three dimensional and physical that it seems far away from software. The multimedia presentation of the design created by Clement Mok is an interesting juxtapostion, with seductive QuickTime movies and an interactive presentation of the information.

It is designed with people in mind.

There is a two stage lift, a tilt limiter and tension adjustment, adjustable lumbar pad and armrests. That combined with three overall sizes makes the design fit the widest range of people so far achieved in office seating.

It fulfills a dream.

The versatility of the anthropometrics is not matched by the image. The robotic insect appearance is demanding, and polarizes people into love and hate. The dream for some is nightmare to others.

It shows the way.

That elastic chain mail material is unique and sets a strong precedent. Herman Miller has patented it and called it the Pellicle, a word that the dictionary defines as "a thin skin or film such as an organic membrane." It is light and tough, it breaths and stretches to give consistent contoured support. It shows us a new alternative to upholstery.

Something excellent.

Bill Stumpf and Don Chadwick have a well earned reputation for seeking excellence. You can tell as soon as you are introduced to this chair that in this case their search has been consistent, thorough, dogged and unambiguous. The excellence will outlast the first shock of the hard soft paradox.

 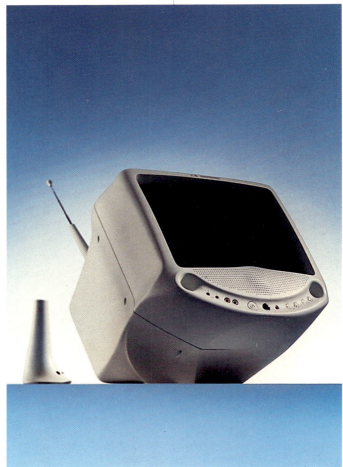

Zéo TV from Thomson
Designed by Philippe Starck

"Objects that Love People": Philippe Starck for Thomson

Philippe Starck is arguably the most influential designer of the 1990s, but we think of him first as an elitist purveyor of high style furniture, environments and traditional products. His work for Thomson (Thomson brands include RCA and General Electric in the U.S., plus Telefunken, Saba and Ferguson in Europe) is an adventure with consumer electronics in the center of the mass market. The first products to be launched in 1993 included Jim Nature under the Saba brand, a TV encased in a housing molded from resin-impregnated wood chips. A new generation is now available including a range for Telefunken and the Zéo television for Thomson. Here's what Starck says:

"Today's industrially manufactured objects are forced to reconsider their legitimacy. Times have changed, and we can no longer produce for the sake of producing. Consequently, objects need to play a double role. They should provide honest service and also send out feelings of friendship and congeniality.

"From now on we've got to create objects that love people... The television object should not exist. To me, it is a totally illegitimate, antiquated object. I imagine television anywhere as a simple beam, a projection into space... That translates into content, but never into container. As we await the extinction of this illegitimate object, we should at least try to make its container send out signs of intelligence and friendship."

It is designed with people in mind.

These are brave words about befriending and even giving love to the audience. Zéo welcomes you with a huge ingenuous grin, badly in need of dental work (although the idea of cables at the front has a convenience), plus a head cocked at an angle or looking attentively upwards.

It fulfills a dream.

Starck fulfills two dreams. One is the influence of his polemic, exemplified above. The other is the originality of his form, that has accelerated away from Modernism, leaving Post-Modernism standing, by an expression of Euclidean geometry modified by both whimsy and the organic force of nature.

It shows the way.

The precedent is divided like the dreams. Ideas like the virtuality of television as a "simple beam, a projection into space" captures the future and fires our imagination. There is also the engaging experiment with form, producing new shapes that have an aesthetic direction worth following.

Something excellent.

The press release of the range of new products from Telefunken is presented in a square box of terra cotta cardboard with the word "excellent" on the outside. Open it and fold back the two layers of tissue paper to reveal an array of electronics looking like chocolates in little crenelated paper cups. A small square booklet under a pull tab labeled "excellent'" has photographs and summary descriptions of the products.

One wonders if the excellence of this ambitious design adventure will flow out into the culture of consumer electronics, or whether it is best left enshrined in the candle in front of a postcard of a painting by Degas in the Royalton Hotel in New York City.

Telefunken - Téléviseur couleur stéréo 55 cm.
Contact presse: Greco - Sandrine Bonamy - 44.82.70.80

**S 352 MSL TV from Telefunken
Designed by Philippe Starck**

RC 1405 remote controller from Telefunken. Designed by Philippe Starck

The S 352 MSL from Telefunken is more sophisticated than appealingly naive, and the friendship is hard to connect with. It looks more like an exercise in surface geometry, transforming from straight line to curve.

Illusion and Reality:
Design Conundrums of the
1990S

R. Craig Miller

FOR MUCH OF THE TWENTIETH CENTURY, the design field has found itself divided into antithetical ideological camps: Beaux Arts vs. Modernism and more recently Modernism vs. Post-Modernism. The 1990s, however, seem to be characterized by an extraordinary blurring of lines which has led to a highly amorphous situation. Perhaps this is due in part simply to the transition from one century to another, as was strongly the case with *fin-de-siècle* design. There are, it seems to me, two more compelling reasons. There is no predominant aesthetic philosophy now, only a myriad of styles that come and go almost like the world of fashion. Moreover, there is no primary design center: Milan's hegemony has for some years been challenged by Spain and Japan, not to mention the recent resurgence of America and France. Late twentieth-century design is, in short, bereft of a strong center core that gives purpose and direction.

For more than 150 years, Western museums have intermittently played an active — and, in many respects, critical — role in the ideological tumult that shapes the design world. In terms of the last four decades per se, European museums have certainly assumed a far more constructive position than their American counterparts. Museums, almost by definition though, have a unique outlook that separates them from design professionals, manufacturers, retailers, and even the press. On the one hand, there is the curators' dichotomy of wishing to be a part of their time and at the same time maintaining a long-term perspective which places them outside of contemporary events. Most importantly, museums have a fundamental and intrinsic preoccupation with aesthetics versus political and social issues, business acumen, or technological innovations, which are certainly important factors but ones that are often quite temporal in nature. This concern with objects as works of art has led to a set of clear parameters which are used by curators in judging designs: questions of form, surface, construction, utility and concept. In short, museums are primarily concerned with issues of philosophy and quality: has an artist sought to address major concepts and to what degree has she or he been successful?

The selection of three objects to represent contemporary design internationally has not been easy. The works presented here are by no means masterworks, for designs of that quality rarely appear even in a decade. Rather these three designs, it seems to me, are symbolic of the contradictory forces now besetting the field. They are objects that aspire to illusions which are in many respects often contrary to their reality. Thus to a remarkable degree these exceptional products reflect the uneasy tenor of our times.

One of the few French architects of international stature today, Jean Nouvel is well known for his "high-tech" design aesthetic. Like Norman Foster and Renzo Piano, his favorite materials are glass and met-

al which he employs in a minimal but highly articulated manner. As a furniture designer, he has produced a small body of work, most notably the "Profils" sofa (1989), the "Elementaire" armchair (1991), and the "Saint James" armchair (1991).

The "Table Less" series (c. 1994) is one of Nouvel's most assured designs, a masterful blending of a myriad of contradictions. It is an industrial object created for a client world-renowned for its traditional luxury products. Moreover, it is intended to be mass-produced but in reality requires an extraordinary degree of handcraftsmanship.

The series was designed for the new building for the Cartier Foundation in Paris. This extraordinary glass-and-metal structure stands like a trans-

Table Less office furniture
Designed by Jean Nouvel

parent Japanese pavilion in a remarkable garden setting within the city. Nouvel completed all of the interiors down to the smallest detail, and these spaces are also a singular achievement in translucency and reflections.

Nouvel completed two furniture designs for the building: "Totum Less," a storage unit, and "Table Less." The latter consists of a desk series and modular table units, which come in two colors (black and gray) and a variety of sizes. The table reflects Nouvel's minimal aesthetic to

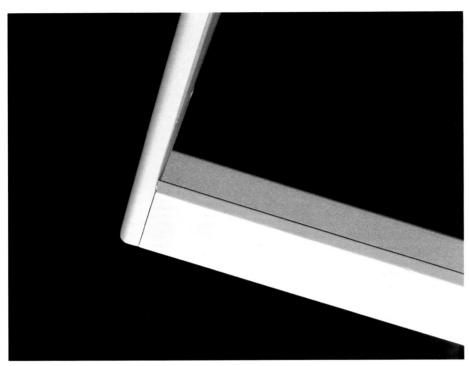

Table Less desk top detail
Designed by Jean Nouvel

reduce everything to its essence. They are simple geometric forms: four L-shaped legs supporting a horizontal plane, all of one material. It is the top, however, which is the *raison d'être* of this design, for Nouvel has sought to give the illusion that this shimmering surface is a single thin sheet; in reality, the table has a complex beveled understructure to provide the required mass for stability. "Table Less" is thus an extraordinary reaffirmation that the pervasive Bauhaus myth of simple geometric forms as the paradigm for industrial production is still very much alive in the 1990s.

Ettore Sottsass represents the antithesis of this Modernist aesthetic. While he has been a major force in Italian design for more than four decades, it was in the last fifteen years that Sottsass's work became synonymous with the Radical (i.e., Post-Modernist) movement through his involvement with such groups as Studio Alchymia and Memphis.

The "Sybilla" vase (1994) is symbolic of the protracted, ambiguous relationship between the decorative object and industry. Indeed, the manufacturer, Sevres, is in this instance a subject of equal importance as the designer and the object in question. This French company was amongst the earliest factories to mass-produce ceramics, achieving renown in the mid-eighteenth century at the beginning of the Modern Movement. Initially sponsored by the monarchy, Sevres subsequently became a state industry, like many other notable European design companies. Sevres has, however, consistently embraced a decorative rather than an industrial aesthetic, although it has a long history of being an innovator in the use of new materials and glazes.

A similar dichotomy is also reflected in the work of Sottsass. Intellectually, he is opposed to the Bauhaus idea of anonymous, mass-produced objects. Rather his work has wide-ranging, overt historical references — Western and Third World, ancient and modern, high art and vernacular — as well as an extraordinarily rich palette of color, materials and patterns. In terms of production, though, Sottsass moves back and forth from industry to craftsman without any qualms, using whichever is most appropriate for the project at hand.

The "Sybilla" vase also is indicative of the power of long traditions — both Sevres and French design — even when dealing with such a forceful designer as Sottsass. This ceramic marks a departure — albeit subtle — from the Italian designer's work over the last decade, which has evolved out of the effusive Memphis aesthetic. In terms of form, the vase consists of two traditional tulip-like urn shapes joined by a connecting stem. A restrained color palette of black, white and orange is used to articulate each part.

Sybilla vase
Designed by Ettore Sottsass

The massive, interlocking geometric shapes are, in short, remarkably chaste and decidedly French, with little of Sottsass's exuberant and seemingly arbitrary compositions. Such refined porcelain forms and glazes, of course, require an extraordinary level of craftsmanship, and this series is available from the Sevres factory only by special order. The "Sybilla" vase thus reaffirms a decorative and industrial tradition now some 250 years old.

Lastly, note should be made of one of the most important forces in terms of form, material and technology on Modern design: engineering. Constantino Dardi, a Roman architect little known in this country, was fascinated with all aspects of technology. His "Principessa" teapot is a compendium of diverse ideas. Following a long tradition of mechanical objects from the Renaissance which amaze and amuse us with their special effects, this design is a late twentieth-century Rube Goldberg feat of engineering realized as a luxury object.

    The teapot, part of the three-piece "Turandot" service, is in essence a miniature building crane. It features a dramatic composition of a semicircular truss balanced on an incised cylindrical base. The tipping of the teapot activates a weight-and-cable system to allow tea to flow out of the spout through an exposed strainer. Made entirely of sterling silver, the "Principessa" requires tour-de-force craftsmanship but, most importantly, an enlightened patron such as Cleto Munari who can commit the time and energy of his Vicenza workshops to achieve such an *objet d'art*. The prototypes were, in fact, only achieved shortly before Dardi's death; Munari has thus far fabricated two examples to order. Feats of engineering, however, do not necessarily have to be industrially manufactured, and Dardi's "Principessa" remains one of the most elegant and fanciful — if perhaps not impractical — examples of metalwork of the 1990s.

    These three objects are thus symbolic of a number of concepts that have played a significant role in shaping Modern design, a movement, which we must constantly remind ourselves, is exceedingly complex and in constant flux. Indeed, it is perhaps the continual reaffirmation of this simple message which is one of the central roles that museums may play in the field of contemporary design: that the world consists of many shades of gray; that there are standards of quality which have informed our civilization generation after generation; and even yet, that the present is never free of the past.

Principessa teapot
Designed by Constantino Dardi

Real Harbingers

Bruce Sterling

Screen shots from World-Wide Web site HotWired
Creative Directors: Barbara Kuhr, John Plunkett
Illustrator: Max Kisman

IT'S QUITE THE HONOR to be asked to critically analyze current design issues for the American Center for Design. Especially since I'm not a designer. I'm a science fiction writer.

I dare not declare what was "good" in design in 1994, since I have no professional criterion for judgment. But I can tell you what has interested me lately. I've picked three significant developments. Real harbingers of some future that no one ever thought would arrive.

The World-Wide Web

The World-Wide Web is a graphic interface for the Internet, the global computer network-of-networks. By every conventional standard of software design, the Web really stinks. It's hard to install. It's difficult to use. It breaks down all the time. Its functions are balky and unpredictable and its malfunctions are deep and shattering. Because it's a layer over the Internet, the Web has not only its own native flaws, but all the inherent flaws of the Internet itself, which are many and terrible.

The Web is nevertheless the sexy spot for net.people in 1994, and its usage during 1994 has increased by something like 33,000%. Why? Because instead of typing hideous UNIX command-line gibberish like "ftp ftp.eff.org get pub/sterling/hacker.crackdown.hqx" you can now point and click. Nice little colored postcards, known as "Web pages," leap up obediently on the screen and do what you ask. More or less. (Quite a bit less, frankly, but the potential's there.)

This development is important to the world of design for three reasons. First, it makes the fantastically powerful and much-hyped Internet into something that the design community can actually use without a two-year short course in the TCP/IP protocol. Second, it makes the

Internet a new global arena for genuine graphic design, and boy is there ever a lot of room for work here. Most Web stuff to date has all the graphic brio of bad assembly instructions. Three, the construction and distribution of World-Wide Web was (and is) a brilliant example of a communitarian, decentralized, globalized, non-commercial design process. The original software was built as a hypertext system for European particle physicists, but it was given away (for free!). Now legions of little gnawing techie termite-artists all over the planet are hacking incremental improvements, and setting up their own Web pages with shrill cries of glee. The World-Wide Web is every single thing that television isn't, and can't ever be. It's also a clear example of how global cyberspace is growing — so quickly, unpredictably and uncontrollably that it really is its own revolution.

PowerBook 540c

As social artifacts, laptop computers are really amazing. It's amazing that a machine of such fantastic complexity and mechanical sophistication can be crammed into such a small box. It's amazing how badly the things actually work in real life. The batteries are a joke. The screens are blurry and speckled with flaws. The keyboards are cramped and squinchy. If you spill coffee in it during a rough flight or bump it off the edge of the hotel bed, you've just ruined $3,500 worth of machinery. Carry a PowerBook in public and it's like pinning a sign to the back of your business suit declaring "Rob Me Please."

PowerBook 540c
Apple Computer, Inc.

It's amazing that after four years of designing the prettiest and friendliest laptops to enormous public acclaim and frenzied consumer demand, Apple Computer still can't manufacture and sell their products efficiently. For months after its introduction, there was a huge backorder on the PowerBook 540c, Apple's current top-of-the-line model.

This machine, the state of the art for 1994, is a whistling dog in almost every way, meaning that what it does is astounding but it doesn't actually do it very well. Its active-matrix color screen is weak, obviously a transitional technology. It doesn't use the current hot chip, the Power-PC chip. Instead, it's sold with a little adhesive sticker on it that promises you can have the new chip someday, a marketing move that would bring a public lynching for anyone but a computer company. It's got an unproven pointing-device, the trackpad. It costs a fortune, yet in 36 months this machine will be so utterly obsolete that if you leave one abandoned on the sidewalk nobody will bother to pick it up. And people love PowerBooks desperately. They dote on them. They'll do most anything to have one. This is a machine that truly is the *sine qua non* of Post-Modern post-industrial society. The computer "industry" is the most genuinely science-fictional enterprise of all time. Just thinking about what they're actually doing to us, to our standards of commerce and value, and to the structure of our society... well, it boggles the mind.

Teva Terradactyl Sport Sandals

Yes, I know that Teva's velcro-strap sandals were actually "designed" — "cobbled together" might be a better term — by a geologist way back in 1983. But this is the year that science fiction writers started wearing them. Tevas have been going through a lot of incremental design improvement since they started as strap-on rubber zoris for the Greenpeace riverboating crowd. Teva Terradactyl sandals in particular have reached some kind of design apotheosis. They now look like something you'd wear while piloting the Buckminster Fuller Dymaxion Car.

Teva Terradactyl Sport Sandals
Deckers Outdoor Corp.

I think it's that system of three little plastic triangles under dynamic tensegrity from the velcro straps that make the look and feel of Tevas so irresistible. The use of multicolored inlays in the sole was a nice velcro-shredding rip-off from the (now flagging) athletic shoe market, but I would surmise that the next design step will be to dump the current graphics on the strap. The fabric straps are still in *faux* Santa Fe style, as if the user were prepared to wade the polluted badlands of the highly saline Colorado. I could go for something rather more highly wired, say cellular-automata checkers or CAD-assisted marble-and-chrome texture-mapping. When this happens, Teva sport sandals will have finally shed their pseudo-green backpacker image to become entirely urban footwear.

It says a lot about our society that Americans are now willing to spend $200 million a year on high-tech hippie sandals. That people walk around nearly barefoot in strap-on gizmos that cost as much as their parents' cordovans. They work, though. The sandals really do work. They feel good, too. They make me feel glad.

II Bellybuttons ...IOI
1642 West 600
North Leesburg, IN 46538

Andrew Blauvelt ...67, 87
209 Taylor Street
Raleigh, NC 27607

Antenna ...62
5402 Rosslyn Avenue
Indianapolis, IN 46220

Art Center College of Design
Design Office ...38, 102, 118
1700 Lida Street
Pasadena, CA 91103

Atlantic Records ...44
75 Rockefeller Plaza
New York, NY 10019

Bates Hori ...68
251 W. 19th St.
New York, NY 10011

Bob's Haus ...124
3728 McKinley Blvd.
Sacramento, CA 95816

BRD Design ...120
6525 Sunset Blvd., 6th Floor
Hollywood, CA 90028

Cahan & Associates ...61, 72
818 Brannan Street, Suite 300
San Francisco, CA 94103

California Institute of the Arts ...34
24700 McBean Parkway
Valencia, CA 91355

Callaway Editions, Inc. ...86
54 Seventh Ave. S.
New York, NY 10014

Charles S. Anderson Design Co. ...69
30 N. First St.
Minneapolis, MN 55401

Chip Kidd Design ...48, 57
201 E. 50th St.
New York, NY 10022

Christopher Vice ...64
47 Bayview Street
Burlington, VT 05401

Coco Raynes Associates Inc. ...41
569 Boylston Street
Boston, MA 02116

Cooper-Hewitt ...56
National Design Museum
2 E. 91st St.
New York, NY 10128

Dave Mason & Associates, Inc. ...83
406-1040 Hamilton Street Vancouver, BC
Canada V6B 2RA

David Carson ...81
128-1/2 10th Street
Del Mar, CA 92014

Design Writing Research ...47, 53, 58
214 Sullivan St.
New York, NY 10012

Duffy Design ...94, III, II2, 134, 135
901 Marquette Ave. S.
Minneapolis, MN 55402

Eastern Michigan University
Department of Art ...30
114 Ford Hall
Ypsilanti, MI 48197

Elixir Design Company ...59
17 Osgood Place
San Francisco, CA 94133

Elliott Peter Earls Design ...121
2 View Street
Greenwich, CT 08630

Fred Bower ...136
7222 Aldgate Lane
Indianapolis, IN 46250

Grady, Campbell Incorporated ...82
920 N. Franklin, Suite 404
Chicago, IL 60610

Irma Boom BV ...49
Louiers Gracht 10
1016 VS Amsterdam
Holland

J. Paul Getty Trust
Publication Services ...88, 92
401 Wilshire Blvd., Suite 850
Santa Monica, CA 90401-1455

Jager Di Paola Kemp Design ...71
308 Pine Street
Burlington, VT 05401

Johnson & Wolverton ...42, 55, 99
1314 NW Irving, Suite 704
Portland, OR 97209

Kode Associates, Inc. ...85
54 W. 22nd St., 4th Floor
New York, NY 10010

Lally Design ...119
603 W. Washington Blvd.
Oak Park, IL 60302

LMNOP ...33
127 S. Harper Ave.
Los Angeles, CA 90048

Louise Sandhaus ...97
24714 Chestnut Street
Newhall, CA 91312

Lowie/Lowrey Design ...76
1225 Abbot Kinney Blvd.
Venice, CA 90291

Rick Poynor is the founder/editor of *Eye*, the London-based international review of graphic design. He is a contributing editor of *Blueprint* magazine and *I.D.*, a columnist for the *AIGA Journal*, and writes for many other publications. His books on design and the visual arts include the critical surveys *Typography Now: The Next Wave* (1991), now in its fifth printing, and *The Graphic Edge* (1993). He is a visiting professor at the Royal College of Art.

Véronique Vienne is a writer, creative director and marketing consultant who lives in Brooklyn, New York. She writes about design, architecture, photography, cultural trends and fashion. Her articles have been published in *Graphis, Print, Metropolis, Eye* and *Communication Arts* as well as general interest magazines and newspapers, including *Mother Jones, Working Woman, Harper's Bazaar, Town & Country, New York Newsday* and the *San Francisco Examiner*.

Stephen Doyle, creative director of the New York firm Drenttel Doyle Partners, brings design and marketing, faux classical typography and commercial necessity into head-on collision. Doyle responds to the city's energy with solutions for *Spy*, the World Financial Center, HarperCollins and other clients that demand to be read. Latest is an identity program for the Cooper-Hewitt Museum, in its new incarnation as the National Design Museum.

As design director of the Walker Art Center, Laurie Haycock Makela is helping to shape this innovative institution's tranformation in the 1990s. While the Walker's graphic language has grown more diverse, in keeping with its multidisciplinary program, communication is the central aim. Haycock Makela's catalog for "In the Spirit of Fluxus" was widely admired. An exhibition she is curating on the design of interactive fiction will open in July 1995.

Rudy VanderLans' *Emigre* magazine began as an outsider's view of the culture he found on arrival from Holland, and despite its success, it still occupies that position. His empathy for experimentation is acute. As editor and designer, he sets out to show and discuss international typography and graphics other publications marginalize or ignore. A ten-year retrospective of Emigre Graphics, *Emigre: Graphic Design Into the Digital Realm*, was published in 1994.

R. Craig Miller is curator in the department of design and architecture at the Denver Art Museum. He has lectured and been published widely, received numerous awards, curated several important exhibitions and served on a number of juries. He presently serves on the advisory boards for Steuben Glass and the Musee des Arts Decoratifs de Montreal.

Bill Moggridge is responsible for formulating strategic directions for IDEO Product Development, an international consultancy with offices in San Francisco, London and Tokyo. Moggridge has contributed to human factors research, pioneered the application of interaction design, and developed a process for the strategic use of design in product innovation.

Bruce Sterling is an author, journalist, editor and critic. He edited the collection *Mirrorshades*, the definitive document of the cyberpunk movement. His non-fiction book *The Hacker Crackdown: Law and Disorder on the Electronic Frontier*, which addresses computer crime and electronic civil liberties, was published by Bantam Books in 1992.

IMAGES

The original images were provided as line art, reflective art or transparencies in one of four sizes;
35mm, 2.25" x 2.25", 4" x 5" or 8" x 10".

INPUT

All images in this book were produced using Kodak Photo CD technology. The transparencies were converted
to Kodak Photo CDs using the Kodak 2200 and 4200 Imaging Workstations. Because Photo CD images are saved in
multiple resolutions, we were able to use an appropriate file for each specific application within the overall
production process.

PAGE COMPOSITION

For the catalog section, position scans were imported into Quark XPress 3.3 for placement, cropping and sizing.
When the page layouts were finalized and approved, finished Quark XPress files were delivered to Moss Printing.

IMAGE PROCESSING

The high resolution Photo CD images were acquired on a KEPS PCS 100 Workstation at Moss Printing, which
consists of a Macintosh Quadra 950 equipped with 200MB of RAM, a SuperMac 20" Trinitron Monitor, a Micronet
1GB Disk Array and a Micronet CD-ROM drive. KEPS PCS 100 hardware and software installed on the Quadra add
Kodak's system calibration, process acceleration, color matching and color separation capabilities to the
Macintosh and Photoshop. The PCS 100 performed automatic color correction of the Photo CD images, and
provided a calibrated viewing environment for user-defined image enhancement. Color correction took place in
Photoshop using PCS 100's accurate monitor preview of the color proofs that were later made to approve
separation quality.

FILM OUTPUT

The Quark XPress files were output using the KEPS Color Server XL, replacing the position scans with
color-corrected high resolution images. High resolution PostScript files were then sent to the Agfa Selectset 5000
imagesetter for final film separations, which were produced at 150 line screen using Kodak Imageset 2000 film
and Kodak processing chemistry. Page films were manually assembled into 16 page signatures to fit the 28" x 40"
printed sheet size.

PROOFING

Electronic Rainbow and film-based four color process Matchprint proofs were used to evaluate color.

PRINTING

The book, its cover and body were printed in-line on Moss Printing's Heidelberg Speedmaster 6/40 offset press
using Kodak Aqua-Image negative printing plates and soy-based four color process inks and spot gloss varnish.
The book was printed on Karma Bright White 80 lb. cover and text, an acid-free premium coated printing paper
from Potlatch Corporation, Northwest Paper Division.

BINDING

The book was perfect bound.

CONTRIBUTORS

American Center for Design thanks the following companies for their generous contributions to
the production of this book.

Moss Printing Company

Potlatch Corporation, Northwest Paper Division

Colophon

BOOK DESIGN AND PHOTOGRAPHY
Rudy VanderLans
Emigre
Sacramento, California

EDITOR
Rob Dewey

FONTS
Matrix, Matrix Bold, Matrix Script Book, Matrix Book Small Caps, Triplex Serif Extra Bold
Designed by Zuzana Licko

PHOTO CREDITS
Page 142
©Photola
Page 143
Tom Vack
Page 150
John Greenleigh, Apple Computer, Inc.